Virginia SOL Grade 6 Reading Secrets

Study Guide

Your Key to Exam Success

Virginia SOL Test Review for the
Virginia Standards of Learning Examination

Dear Future Exam Success Story:

Congratulations on your purchase of our study guide. Our goal in writing our study guide was to cover the content on the test, as well as provide insight into typical test taking mistakes and how to overcome them.

Standardized tests are a key component of being successful, which only increases the importance of doing well in the high-pressure high-stakes environment of test day. How well you do on this test will have a significant impact on your future- and we have the research and practical advice to help you execute on test day.

The product you're reading now is designed to exploit weaknesses in the test itself, and help you avoid the most common errors test takers frequently make.

How to use this study guide

We don't want to waste your time. Our study guide is fast-paced and fluff-free. We suggest going through it a number of times, as repetition is an important part of learning new information and concepts.

First, read through the study guide completely to get a feel for the content and organization. Read the general success strategies first, and then proceed to the content sections. Each tip has been carefully selected for its effectiveness.

Second, read through the study guide again, and take notes in the margins and highlight those sections where you may have a particular weakness.

Finally, bring the manual with you on test day and study it before the exam begins.

Your success is our success

We would be delighted to hear about your success. Send us an email and tell us your story. Thanks for your business and we wish you continued success-

Sincerely,

Mometrix Test Preparation Team

TABLE OF CONTENTS

Reading Assessment

Root word and affix

A root word is the original word, before it is added onto. An affix is a prefix, infix, or suffix that is added onto a root word. Many affixes in the English language come from Latin or Greek origins. A prefix is added at the beginning of a root word, an infix, to the middle, and a suffix to the end of a root word. By looking at the meaning of a root word and the meaning of any affixes added to the root word, the reader can figure out the approximate meaning of the word. For example, the root word 'like' means to enjoy. The prefix 'dis-' means not. The reader can therefore say that the word 'dislike' means to not enjoy.

Example
Determine the meaning of the word 'prepay' by using knowledge of root words and affixes.

A reader can use root words and affixes to figure out the general meaning of an unknown word. Knowing root words and affixes is helpful on tests where analogies are made using unfamiliar words. By figuring out the general meaning of an unknown word, a tester can figure out the general relationship between two words.

In the word 'prepay', the root word 'pay' means to give, such as to give money for goods or services. The prefix 'pre-' means before. The full word 'prepay' therefore means to give money before goods or services are granted. A person might prepay for a class, an appointment, or to reserve an item that has not arrived at the store yet.

Context clues

The term *context clues* refers to words or phrases found in the sentences surrounding an unknown. Context clues may include examples of the new word, synonyms, antonyms, definitions, or contrasting information. By using context clues in the surrounding sentences, the reader can determine approximately what the word means. A context clue in the form of an example may contain the words including 'such as', a dash, or a colon before stated information. A synonym is a word with a meaning similar to the unknown word, where an antonym is a word with a meaning opposite to the unknown word. A definition will state exactly what the new word means and contrasting information will include facts that are different from the new word.

Example 1
Read the following sentence and determine the meaning of the word 'pattering' based on context clues.
"I like you! I like you!" she cried out, pattering down the walk; and she chirped and tried to whistle, which last she did not know how to do in the least. (From The Secret Garden by Frances Hodgson Burnett)

Context clues are key words within a sentence that help the reader to find the meaning of an unknown word. In the example sentence, the words 'down the walk' show that the character is moving on a sidewalk. The reader knows that the character is crying out and trying to chirp and whistle while moving, so the character cannot be completely out of breath. The character is also trying to reach the person or thing that she is crying out to. From these context clues, the reader can guess that the word 'pattering' means to walk quickly.

Example 2
Using context clues, determine the meaning of the word 'pestilent' in the following sentence.

In fact, he declared it was of no use to work on his farm; it was the most pestilent little piece of ground in the whole country; everything about it went wrong, and would go wrong in spite of him. (From Rip Van Winkle by Washington Irving).

Context clues are words in the sentence and surrounding sentences that help the reader to figure out the meaning of an unknown word. In the example, the word 'pestilent' is used to describe the ground. The character states that it was of no use to work on his farm and that everything about it went wrong. This indicates that the ground was difficult to work with, since the character had trouble with the ground no matter what he tried ('and would go wrong in spite of him'). The reader can assume, from these observations, that the word 'pestilent' means troublesome, annoying, or not allowing anything to grow, since this example is about the ground on a farm.

Use of analogies
Analogies help the reader to see a relationship between a word or idea that is known and a new word or idea. An analogy may show that the new, unknown word is a synonym, antonym, or has a degree of relation to the known word or idea. In addition, an analogy may show that the new word is a part of the known word, a type of the known word, or is a use of the known word. An analogy may show cause and effect between an unknown word and a known word, as well as show relative size. Analogies help the reader to figure out the meaning of a new word and show something in common. For example, an analogy may compare the relation alligator: reptile. An alligator is a type of reptile. An equivalent analogy may be that of chicken: bird.

Denotative and connotative meanings

The denotative meaning of a word is the exact dictionary definition of the word. The connotative meaning of a word is the emotion conveyed by the use of the word in context. The word may have associated meaning in addition to its dictionary definition. For example, the word 'home' is defined in the dictionary as a place where a person or people live. When a reader sees the word in the following context: "Marisol walked briskly home, where the smell of fresh-baked apple pie wafted through the warm kitchen," the reader will associate the meaning of the word with coziness and a feeling of well-being. The connotative meaning of a word in a passage can be found by looking at the context clues.

Example
Determine the connotative meaning of the word 'ancient' in the following sentence. Amy pulled an *ancient* calculator out of the desk, and sat down to figure out how to use it.

The denotative meaning of a word is the actual dictionary definition of the word. The connotative meaning of a word is implied or suggested by the word and may have emotions associated with it. In the example, the word 'ancient' literally means very old. The connotative meaning of the word ancient suggests that the calculator does not work as well as more modern versions. In technology, ancient is relative to what is currently being used. For example, a computer may be out of date in a couple years, whereas an ancient society may date back several thousand years.

Information in play vs. in a news story

The information in a play is presented according to acts and lines said by each character. When written, a play will start each line with the name of the character stating that line. Information that is not stated by the characters but meant to be known by the audience is stated in italics before the play opens, sometimes read by a narrator at the beginning. Also, stage directions are often noted in parentheses in a written play. In a news story, information is most commonly in paragraph format. The most important information is stated at the beginning, that way, the reader knows immediately what the story is about and the key points that the author wishes to convey.

Idioms

Idioms differ from the literal English meaning of words in the fact that they are expressions, or common ways of saying something. For example, 'to keep tabs on' is an idiomatic expression that is commonly used to communicate to someone to closely watch someone or something. Based on experience, determine the meaning of the idiom in the following sentence:

> Jared *hung his head* after viewing his score on the test and realizing that he had not studied the material long enough.

In the example, the phrase 'hung his head' is an idiom that means to look down with shame. By reading the rest of the sentence, the reader can see that the character did not study enough, which would lead him to be upset about his score on the test. Idioms can be figured out through the use of context clues, but are also learned through experience with the language.

Plot

The term 'plot' refers to the series of events that take place in a story. The events in a story may take place in one location, or many locations. A story may take place in a short amount of time, or

over many years. Every story is different. A story always has to start somewhere, however. The first event in a story signals the beginning of the plot. Two characters may be simply talking at the opening of a story, which is the first step in the plot of the story. The characters may then hear a loud noise and rush outdoors, which is the next event that takes place in the plot of the story. Stories may vary in length from half a page to novel-length, but they all follow a progression of events that the author winds together to form the plot.

Main conflict

Example 1
Read the following sentence from The Call of the Wild by Jack London and describe the main conflict in the sentence. Explain how the conflict may be resolved.

> The breaking down of discipline likewise affected the dogs in their relations with one another.

Based on the information in the sentence, an event has caused the dogs, the characters in the story, to not follow their regular routine. The sentence indicates that there has been a breaking down of discipline which is affecting how the dogs relate to each other. In order to solve this conflict, discipline needs to be restored. However, in order to return to previous relations between the dogs, any problems that are in the way of conflict resolution need to be taken care of. The word likewise means also, which tells the reader that other avenues are being affected in the story besides the relations between the dogs.

Example 2
Read the following sentence and explain the main conflict between the two characters:

> Joe stared angrily at Jamie's retreating back as

Jamie raced away down
the field with Joe's soccer
ball.

The main conflict in the sentence is that Jamie has Joe's soccer ball. There may be additional conflicts between the two characters, but none are evident from the evidence shown in the sentence. In any story, a conflict may be minor and only affect part of the story, or be the main focus, taking an entire story to solve a conflict between characters. In the context of the sentence, it is not clear whether or not the entire story will revolve around Jamie taking Joe's soccer ball. However, the current conflict is based upon that information in the sentence.

Problem resolution

The term 'problem resolution' in reference to a story means that a solution to a situation or issue has been found. The solution may have come about through direct action by characters in the story, or the situation may have been resolved by outside means. The problem in the story may have been a key conflict between characters, or it may have been part of a bigger issue. For example, two characters may be trying to decide whether to go to the park in the evening. If the park is closed due to bad weather, it solves the problem for the two characters. However, the characters may still need to decide what to do in the evening. Now that they cannot go to the park, they need to come up with a different plan. The author of a story uses problem resolution to show progression of events in a story.

Character trait

The traits of a character may include how they act and physical characteristics, that are unique to a specific character. For example, a character may be outgoing, which means he or she likes to talk a lot,

or have bright red hair. These are both character traits.

An author uses character traits to describe a character in a story. Character traits help the reader to learn more about how the character acts and what they look like. By comparing the different character traits in a story, the reader can see similarities and differences between characters. The author includes character traits to help the reader understand why a character may act a certain way in the story. For example, a character who is shy may not want to talk with a lot of people in a new classroom, but a character who is outgoing may want to talk with many.

An author typically provides many details about a character so that the reader can learn more about the character's motivations, relationships, and any conflicts they may have in the story. The traits of a character may also include how they act and how they look. Characters are often motivated by things that have already happened in their life or how they feel about a topic. The author will often give the reader enough information about the character so that the reader can figure out why the character responds to a situation in a certain way. The author will also often give details about the relationships between characters and points they may conflict on. For example, a character may be good friends with another character; however, the two characters may disagree on where to play outside if one character likes being near the water and the other character does not.

Points of view

An author may use first, second, or third person point of view in a text. First person point of view is written from the perspective of one character. Use of the pronouns 'I', 'me', 'we', and 'my' indicate that the author is using first person point of view. Second person point of view uses the pronoun 'you' when telling the story to another person. Second person point of view is the least commonly used point of view. Third person point of view tells a story from an all-knowing, or omniscient, perspective. The reader can get into the thoughts and points of view of multiple characters in a story when third person point of view is used.

Limitations of first person
First person point of view is told from the perspective of only one person. Since this is the case, the reader only gets one side of the story, without any other angles on what may have happened in the text, such as in a personal narrative. For example, the book *The Catcher in the Rye* is told from a first person point of view, that of Holden Caulfield. Alternately, the third person point of view gives a more objective, or whole, view of a story as it is viewed and told from many different perspectives. With this, the reader often knows what is going on in the mind of each character in the story.

Conclusion

The conclusion of a text is typically found in the last one or two paragraphs of the text. A conclusion wraps-up the text and reminds the reader of the main point of the text. The conclusion is the author's way of leaving the reader with a final note to remember about the paper and comes after all the supporting points of the text have been presented. For example, a paper about the importance of avoiding too much sunlight may have a conclusion that reads: By limiting sun exposure to 15 minutes a day and wearing sunscreen of at least SPF 15, a person can reduce their risk of getting skin cancer later in life.

Opposite point of view of topic sentence

Read the following topic sentence. Describe what the opposite point of view would include.

> The new bike path at Primer School provides families in the community with a safe opportunity to get some fresh air on the weekends.

This topic sentence could be taken in several different directions. The main focus of the sentence is that the bike path is safe and allows for families to get out and enjoy some fresh air on the weekends. The opposite point of view may state that the new bike path is unsafe and the air is polluted. An example of a topic sentence with the opposite point of view may state: The new bike path at Primer School is unsafe for families in the community to travel on the weekends and goes through a polluted area.
When looking for the main point in a sentence, look for keywords that define the sentence. In the sentence about the bike path, we know that the path is new, seems safe, and has fresh air. By changing around these keywords, the entire meaning of the sentence can be shifted.

Main idea and supporting details

The main idea(s) in a passage are usually located in the first paragraph or two of text. Having the main idea(s) near the beginning of the passage allows the author to grab the reader's attention and let him or her know what the rest of the passage will discuss. To find the main idea(s) in a passage, the read should ask questions while reading, such as "What is this passage about? What does the author want the reader to know about the topic?" The supporting details will provide evidence that the main idea(s) is/are correct. Supporting details are found in the body of a passage. The supporting details often provide examples of the main idea. For example, a passage may contain the main idea: "Ellis Island was an entry-point to America for many immigrants during the Industrial Revolution." A supporting detail for this main idea may be "Immigrants were examined for contagious diseases at Ellis Island before being granted entry to America."

Example 1
Determine the main idea that the following sentence tells the reader. Indicate what details support the main idea.

> Her breath billowed out in clouds of white and disappeared into the quiet air.

The main idea is what the author wants the reader to understand about the text, with details to help to explain or support it. A main idea usually states the point of an entire essay, article, or book, but a main idea can be simply stated in one sentence. The main idea in the sentence above is that a girl is outside in the cold. Details to support this include the word 'her', showing that the character is a girl, and 'clouds of white', which indicate that the air is cold. In order to conclude that the girl is out in the cold, the reader needs to understand that breath can be seen when the air is cold.

Example 2
Decide whether the following sentence is the main point or a supporting point of a text. State where the information would be placed in an outline.

> One type of horseback riding, bareback horseback riding, involves sitting on a moving horse without a saddle and grasping the horse's mane.

This sentence is a supporting point, with the main point of the entire text most likely about horseback riding in general. As a supporting point, this sentence would go further down in an outline, next to any numeral after numeral I. This sentence can be followed by additional sub-points that further explain the concept of bareback horseback riding. When a supporting point is used to clarify a main point or topic, the supporting point helps to break the topic down into smaller pieces.

Summarization and organization of information

The reader of a passage may wish to take notes to provide an overall summary of the text when they are finished. On the test, a column may be provided for "My notes about what I am reading." This allows the reader to recall important facts about each paragraph. A note may be a few words indicating the main idea of the paragraph. In addition to note-taking, information from a passage may be summarized and organized using the following:
- An outline
- A mind-map (has a central main idea, with branches connecting to supporting details)
- A spider-map (has a main idea at the top, with supporting details branching downwards)
- A summary paragraph
- A Venn diagram or other graphic organizer (is a graph that allows ideas to overlap or simply be displayed in a visual manner)

Paraphrasing and summarizing

Paraphrasing involves stating the text in the reader's own words, while keeping the original meaning of the text. Summarizing involves stating main points of the text clearly and to-the-point. Paraphrasing takes all of the original

- 6 -

ideas and words them in a way that the reader can better understand them. Summarizing takes information and states it simply, in a much more succinct form. Both paraphrasing and summarizing allow the reader to remember main points explained in the text. Summarizing puts information in a short form that keeps the main points of the whole text. In other words, paraphrasing is often done for individual ideas, while summarizing is done for an entire block of text or ideas.

Flashback, symbolism, and foreshadowing

Flashback occurs when the author of a story tells the reader events or thoughts that occurred in the past, helping the reader to make sense out of events that are currently happening in the story. Symbolism is when the author uses one object to stand for something else. For example, the author may include a flag flying high throughout a story to show pride in the characters' country and togetherness. Foreshadowing gives the reader hints that an event will occur. For example, the author may indicate that a character feels nervous and is unprepared for a competition, which can tell the reader that the character may not do well when the competition occurs. On the other hand, if the character feels confident and is well-prepared for a competition, the reader can guess that the character will do fairly well in the competition.

Example 1
Read the following sentence from Black Beauty by Anna Sewell and state the type of literary device used in the sentence:
> The first place that I can well remember was a large pleasant meadow with a pond of clear water in it.

The sentence contains the literary device 'flashback.' The character in the story is remembering back, which gives the reader some background information about the character. The character remembers a field with clear water and describes the field as a large pleasant meadow. This indicates that the character enjoyed the field and did not have bad memories of the location. By looking at the wording used in each sentence, the reader can figure out how the character feels about the information revealed in a flashback.

Example 2
Read the following sentence from The Red Badge of Courage by Stephen Crane. State the character traits that the reader learns from the sentence.
> He remembered how he had stood, a small, thrillful boy, prepared to follow the dingy lady upon the white horse, or the band in its faded chariot.

The sentence is part of a flashback within the story, which gives the reader information about how the character used to be. The information in the sentence indicates that the character was a small boy. The word 'thrillful' indicates that he was eager and amazed by a parade at the time. The flashback is not unpleasant, it just indicates a different time period and perception. A flashback is often used to show contrast to current feelings or how a character may be led to feel a certain way about a current situation. The author's inclusion of the sentence indicates that the boy has changed over time, most likely physically grown as well as in his perception of events over time.

Example 3
Read the following sentence from Call of the Wild by Jack London and state what type of literary device is used in the sentence:

Buck did not read the
newspapers or he would
have known that trouble
was brewing, not alone for
himself, but for every
tidewater dog, strong of
muscle and with warm,
long hair, from Puget
Sound to San Diego.

This sentence includes the literary device called foreshadowing, which is used to indicate that something will happen in the future. In the sentence, foreshadowing is used to show that something will happen to the dog in the story. The author indicates that trouble was brewing and that the dog, along with 'every tidewater dog, strong of muscle and with warm, long hair, from Puget Sound to San Diego' will be susceptible to the same event that is about to occur. None of the dogs know about the event that will occur, of course, but the author places this information into the sentence to let the reader know that something will happen.

Example 4
Read the following sentence from "The Legend of Sleepy Hollow" by Washington Irving and explain what literary device is used in the sentence:
    The whole neighborhood
    abounds with local tales,
    haunted spots, and
    twilight superstitions;
    stars shoot and meteors
    glare more often across
    the valley than in any
    other part of the country.

The literary device of symbolism is used in the sentence. The phrase 'stars shoot and meteors glare more often across the valley than in any other part of the country' is used to symbolize the strange atmosphere of the location. The presence of more shooting stars and meteors is meant to indicate that something out of the ordinary is going on in the setting of

the story. An author will often use symbolism to take ordinary objects and give them additional meaning. In this sentence, symbolism gives a questioning, ethereal tone to the setting that may not otherwise be achieved.

Purpose

A text may be written to inform the reader on a topic that they did not previously know about, as many non-fiction texts are. A text may express an opinion on a topic, containing evidence to back-up the author's point-of-view. A text can also be written to influence the reader to think a certain way about a topic, calling the reader to take action on the topic, or point the reader toward resources to learn more about the topic. A text may be written simply to entertain the reader, as many fictional stories are.

Example 1
Read the following sentence from Morte d'Arthur by Sir Thomas Malory. State the author's purpose in writing the sentence; whether it is to inform, entertain, persuade, or state an opinion.
    But Arthur was still only a
    baby, not two years old,
    and Merlin knew it would
    be no use yet to proclaim
    him king.

The purpose of the sentence is to entertain the reader. The sentence does not tell the reader important information about a specific topic, it is simply used as part of a greater fictional story meant for entertainment. The sentence does not persuade the reader to accept a certain point of view, nor does it state an opinion.

When an author wishes to persuade the reader to accept a certain point of view, evidence is used to back-up a claim. If the author wants to state an opinion, that opinion is included within the text. Sentences that are meant to inform contain facts that the reader needs to know and are not often found in a fictional stories.

<u>Example 2</u>
Read the following sentence. State the author's point in writing the sentence, whether it is to inform, entertain, persuade, or state an opinion:

> The new city law makes it
> illegal to use cell phones
> to send text messages
> while driving.

The purpose of this sentence is to inform the reader. The sentence does not state an opinion on the topic, nor is it meant to entertain the reader. The sentence also does not persuade the reader to accept a certain point of view. The sentence gives information to the reader that they need to know in order to avoid breaking the law.

Organization

The information from a text, whether it is a fictional or factual story, can be organized using one of the following means:

- An outline
- A timeline
- A graphic organizer (including mind-maps, spider-maps, Venn diagrams, or a variety of creative graphic organizers)

A reader may take notes in the margin of a text as he or she is reading, including key points that the reader needs to remember. For example, the reader may jot down the main idea of the selection, then the main idea of each supporting paragraph. If important information such as a supporting statistic is included in the text, the reader may jot that down in the margin as well. The reader will then take all of the information and place it in an outline, timeline, or graphic organizer. A timeline will place important facts in

chronological order, whereas the other means of organization will place information in order of importance or order that it occurs in the text.

Text structure

<u>Cause and effect</u>
The term *cause and effect* means when one event happens in a text, another event occurs because of it. The term *chronology* refers to the order of events over time. For example, a text may discuss the school policy that, when a student is late to school too many times, they receive a detention. The student being late too many times is the cause and the detention is the effect. Chronology of events in a story can occur over a short, or extended, period of time. For example, if a text discusses the rise of the Roman Empire, it may include the rulers of the Roman Empire over time and any changes that occurred during each ruler's time in power.

Example: Identify the text structure that is used in the following sentence from Morte d'Arthur by Sir Thomas Malory:

> The king had given his
> promise, so he was
> obliged to agree.

The text structure of cause and effect is used in this sentence. The cause in the sentence is that the king gave his promise, and the effect is that he had to agree. Information can also be organized according to chronological order, spatial order, order of importance, or organized by description. Chronological order means the order of events as they occur over time. Spatial order is the way things are placed in a location, such as the way people are seated around a table. Order of importance is used to place the most important information first, with the least important information last (or vice-versa). Description is used to organize

- 9 -

information according to what it looks and feels like.

Description example
State the text structure used in the following sentence from A Tramp Abroad by Mark Twain:

> He was a middle-aged, simple-hearted miner who had lived in a lonely corner of California among the woods and mountains a good many years, and had studied the ways of his only neighbors, the beasts and birds, until he believed he could accurately translate any remark which they made.

Description is used in the sentence to present the character of the miner. The reader learns that the miner is middle-aged, simple-hearted, lived in the woods and mountains of California for many years, and extensively studied nature. This gives the readers clues about where the character came from and, based on his background, what he may think about certain topics. For example, the miner lived amongst nature, so he may think that it is important to respect both flora and fauna. The text structure gives the reader important background information that can set the stage for later events in the story.

Style, tone, and mood

An author can vary the feel of a text by changing the style, tone, and mood of each sentence. The style of a text refers to whether the author uses long, flowing sentences, short, choppy sentences, or something in-between. The text may be organized in short lines, short paragraphs, or long paragraphs. The tone of a paper helps to establish the mood of the text. Tone involves the attitude that the author displays in the paper. For

example, the author may feel exuberant about a sunny day, but feel down on a gloomy day. The words that the author uses to describe the scene and situation in the story help to define its tone. The mood of a story may be uplifting, down, scared, or excited, again, depending upon the words the author uses. All of these elements: style, tone, and mood, can affect how the reader feels about the story.

Example 1
Describe the tone of the following sentence from "The Adventure of the Speckled Band" by Sir Arthur Conan Doyle:

> Then creeping up to me and making a trumpet of his hand, he whispered into my ear again so gently that it was all that I could do to distinguish the words.

The tone of the sentence is mysterious. The words "creeping" and "whispered into my ear" make the reader wonder why the character needs to be quiet in the story. The characters in the sentence seem to be waiting for something to happen, making the reader may feel that they need to hold their breath while waiting to see what happens to the characters in the story. The tone of the sentence is appropriately mysterious, since the story is written as a mystery. By creating suspense in the text, the author makes the reader want to see what happens next.

Example 2
Describe the style and mood of the following sentence from The Adventures of Tom Sawyer by Mark Twain:

> He surveyed the fence, and all gladness left him and a deep melancholy settled down upon his spirit.

The style of the sentence is fully descriptive of the character's feelings, painting a picture in the reader's mind of the character's thoughts. The author uses the word 'and' twice to signify the sinking spirits of the character in the sentence. The mood of the sentence mirrors the emotion of the character, as the character goes from level-headed to quite sad, from which the reader can deduce that the character does not want to do something, which has brought down his mood as a result. In this particular scenario, the character does not want to spend a long time whitewashing a fence while he had other plans on such a beautiful day. The style of the sentence is direct; it explains how the character feels in the story.

Text evidence

The term *text evidence* refers to information included in a text that supports the main point of the paper. A reader can draw conclusions or generalizations based upon information found in a text, in which the author will deliberately include key points that serve as supporting details for the main point. For example, the main point of a paper may state: The average yearly rainfall in the city has risen by 2 inches per year since 1999. The paper would go on to include the amount of rainfall for each month or season and any contributing factors that may be causing an increase in yearly rainfall. Additional facts, or text evidence to support the point that yearly rainfall is rising in the city would help to prove that the author's main point is correct.

Drawing a conclusion

Draw a conclusion based on the following sentence from The Adventures of Tom Sawyer by Mark Twain:
> He had discovered a great
> law of human action,
> without knowing it—

> namely, that in order to
> make a man or a boy covet
> a thing, it is only necessary
> to make the thing difficult
> to attain.

The reader can conclude from the sentence that the character did not set out to learn something, but through an action, the character learned that people will want what is hard to attain. The character learned a fact about human nature; that a person will value something more if they have to work hard for it than if it is simply given to them. The word *covet* means to desire, which the character learns can be manipulated by making an item or an outcome more difficult to grasp. In everyday life, this could apply toward taking a hard test and doing well. If someone studies for a hard test and does well, the person will value their score more than if the test was very easy and he or she did not study for the test.

Fact and opinion

When deciding whether information is fact or opinion, a reader needs to look at whether or not the information is well-accepted by experts, in addition to being backed-up by outside sources. A fact is something that is true, regardless of what the author thinks, on the contrary, an opinion is what the author thinks, without regard to evidence to back-up that claim. For example, for a paper about caves, a fact may read: Extensive cave systems run through the soft limestone of Central Texas. An opinion may read: Caving, also called spelunking, is an enjoyable recreational activity. It is a fact that caves run throughout Central Texas, but it is the author's opinion that spelunking is an enjoyable recreational activity.

<u>Example</u>
Decide whether the following sentence is a fact or opinion. Explain your reasoning.

The new school year will start one week before Labor Day and end on May 31st.

This sentence is a fact. The school calendar is set each year to start and finish on a certain day and while days are built into the schedule to account for bad weather, right now, the school year is set to end on May 31st. The information is factual because it is established by the school district. An opinion would express a personal feeling about the situation. For example, in the sentence, an opinion might state: The new school year should start after Labor Day and end the second week in June, so that students have the full month of August for summer.

Organization of ideas in text

Authors organize ideas through cause and effect, chronological order, comparison and contrast, inductively, and deductively. In addition, an author may organize ideas using spatial order, order of importance, and description. Cause and effect shows that one event leads to another. Chronological order places events in order by the time in which they occurred. Comparison and contrast involves showing similarities and differences between items or events. To organize ideas inductively, an author states detailed facts, then more general principles. To organize ideas deductively, an author lists general ideas, then gets more specific. Spatial order involves organizing ideas by their place in a space, such as a room.

Organizing ideas by order of importance places the most important idea first and the least important idea last, or vice-versa. An author can also use description of ideas or events to place them in a logical order.

Example
Read the following sentence. Decide how the author has organized ideas.
> The moonlight shone upon the lake in tongs of glowing white, reflecting off the water so that the path in front of the canoe could be seen without a flashlight.

The sentence uses description and cause and effect for organization. The moonlight reflecting off the water is the cause, with the effect being the person or persons in the canoe being able to see in front of the canoe without a flashlight. The author describes the scene in detail, so that the reader can picture a moonlit lake with a canoe gliding along the water. Other forms of organization that the author could have used, but did not, include comparison and contrast, order of importance, spatial order, chronological order, inductive organization, and deductive organization of ideas.

Memoirs and personal narratives

A memoir is a form of literature where the author tells about only a specific part of his life. Memoirs do not tell the author's story from birth to old age. They are often written by people in politics or in business, and tell about the author's career and successes.

A personal narrative is most often the first type of writing a person will do. In a personal narrative the author tells a story about his life. It can contain as much detail, dialogue, and excitement as the author wants to put into it. Personal narratives are often more entertaining because they are very personal.

Both memoirs and personal narratives are types of autobiographical works. They are written about the author to tell others about the author's life and

- 12 -

experiences. The main difference is that autobiographies focus on the whole of the author's life, instead of focusing only on small parts of it.

Rule of three and the magic helper

The rule of three is based on the assumption that things that come in threes are more entertaining, funnier, and more effective than any other number. Research shows that the reader can better absorb ideas within the literature if they are grouped into threes. For example, many stories group characters into groups of three. There are stories about the three little pigs, Goldilocks and the three bears, and the three blind mice. Authors will also often use the number three within the story where a character has to complete three tasks or complete an action three times.

The magic helper is an element often used when the main character must accomplish a daunting or even an impossible task. The main character may receive aid from a fairy godmother, a genie, or just a person with a special skill or power, who makes the previously difficult or impossible task doable. The helper is usually with the character during all the challenges in the story.

Television and printed media

Television is one of many media used to affect a person's emotions, and also behavior. Different images, words, graphics, and sounds can be used to create meaning. For example, advertisements directed at children will often show other kids having fun doing an activity. The bright colors and obvious excitement on their faces will entice a child watching the advertisement to want the item. The child sees other kids having

fun, and wants to have fun too. Adults can be influenced by media in much the same way.

Journalists will write positive stories about a person or product that encourages the adult to want to try a product or back a certain person because of the results they read about. Images can also be used to appeal to a person's emotions. A sad image such as a neglected animal or a starving child will often result in compassion from the viewer and can even spur the viewer to some action, such as donating money to a cause.

Paraphrasing

Paraphrasing occurs when a reader puts ideas into his or her own words. If every word in the example sentence was copied, the sentence would not be a paraphrase; it would be a direct quotation. Paraphrasing keeps the main idea of a sentence, paragraph, or story, but uses the reader's own words.

Example
Paraphrase the following sentence:
> August was the hottest month of the year in Mississippi, a time when people stayed indoors and drank lemonade.

An example of this sentence paraphrased is: People drank lemonade indoors during August, the hottest month in Mississippi. Note that the same information is contained in both the original sentence and the paraphrased sentence, but the wording is different. Paraphrasing is a good technique to use when taking notes from a story, to help with understanding the main ideas that are presented.

Practice Test #1

Practice Questions

Questions 1 – 12 pertain to the following short story:

A World of White: The Iditarod Trail

(1) Imagine clinging desperately to your sled as brutal winds batter your body. The path ahead appears and disappears like a mirage, frequently obscured by blowing curtains of snow. You are freezing and sweating at the same time. Your throat burns with thirst, and your body aches with fatigue. You know your dogs must feel it too, so you encourage them to press on to the next checkpoint. All around you, the world is endless, empty, and white. Welcome to the Iditarod Trail.

(2) Alaska's Iditarod Trail is the world's most famous sled dog racing venue. But the trail is older than the sport of sled dog racing. In fact, the Iditarod Trail was first established in the early 1900s, during the Alaskan gold rush. In those days, dog teams were used for work, hauling thousands of pounds of gold from landlocked Iditarod to the port of Anchorage. But in faraway Nome, also known for gold, six-year-old George Allen had the idea to put together a race to see whose sled dogs were fastest, and the sport of sled dog racing was born.

(3) Though the Iditarod Trail race is the most famous race in the sport of sled dog racing, the first race along the trail was actually a race to save lives. In 1925, a diphtheria outbreak began in Nome. To prevent an epidemic that could kill thousands, doctors were desperate for the vaccine serum, but the closest serum was in Anchorage. The train ran from Anchorage to the village of Nenana, but that was still 674 miles from Nome. A cry for help was sent by the doctors, and in the midst of the blizzards and windstorms of January, the call was answered. Twenty brave mushers drove their dogs in a frantic relay, carrying 300,000 bottles of serum from Nenana to Nome. They followed the Iditarod Trail.

(4) Dog sledding, or "mushing," became quite popular after that heroic journey, but by the 1960s, it had lost popularity and the Iditarod Trail had been largely forgotten. There were a few lovers of mushing, however, who worked tirelessly to reestablish the Iditarod Trail and create a new sled dog race that used the trail as its course. The first official race was held in 1967 to celebrate the centennial of the purchase of Alaska from Russia. The race involved 58 drivers who mushed 56 miles in two days. This race was a success, but the popularity and future of the Iditarod Trail was still in question.

(5) In March of 1973, the first Anchorage to Nome Iditarod Trail race was organized and held. This race was much longer than previous races, covering more than 1,000 miles—the whole Iditarod Trail. Thirty-four mushers began the race, but only 22 were able to finish. After the 1973 race, the popularity of the Iditarod Trail finally grew and was firmly established. In 1978, the Iditarod Trail became a National Historic Trail.

- 14 -

(6) The modern Iditarod Trail race is open to mushers over 18 years old who have qualified in a recognized race of 200 miles or more. For younger mushers between 14 and 18 years old, the Junior Iditarod offers a 130-mile version of the race. Many Junior Iditarod participants go on to compete in the Iditarod Trail race, as the Junior Iditarod is good practice for the grueling trek of the main race. All mushers must prepare for the race extensively, often for months before the race. Many mushers run their dogs more than 1,500 miles in preparation, giving them experience in all types of weather and terrain.

(7) To enter the Iditarod Trail race, participants must pay an entrance fee. Then they must travel to Anchorage with their dogs. In Anchorage, they attend a mushers' banquet where they are given their racing order numbers. Afterwards, all participating dogs are checked by a veterinarian and marked by race officials to prevent dog switching mid-race, which is not allowed. The dogs are even drug tested at the beginning and at checkpoints throughout the race to prevent cheating! Finally, the sleds and equipment are checked. Then participants are ready to start the race.

(8) On the morning of the Iditarod Trail race, mushers leave Anchorage in their assigned racing order. They are sent out one at a time, at two-minute intervals. For more than a week—sometimes up to three weeks—they travel throughout Alaska, stopping at designated checkpoints all along the Iditarod Trail as they make their way to Nome. When all participants have reached Nome, another mushers' banquet is held. Awards are given, and everyone is applauded for their achievement. Win or lose, the mushers know that only the toughest of the tough have what it takes to finish the race and conquer the great Iditarod Trail.

1. What does the simile in paragraph 1 describe?
   a. The snow
   b. The path
   c. The musher's throat
   d. The dogs

2. What does "landlocked" mean in paragraph 2?
   a. Barricaded by hills
   b. Built underground
   c. Not on a waterway
   d. In the mountains

3. What two cities are on the ends of the Iditarod Trail?
   a. Anchorage and Nome
   b. Nome and Nenana
   c. Iditarod and Anchorage
   d. Nenana and Iditarod

4. What is the author's main purpose in writing this article?
   a. To encourage mushers to race on the Iditarod Trail
   b. To inform the reader about the 1925 diphtheria outbreak
   c. To describe the terrain of Alaska
   d. To educate the reader about the Iditarod Trail

- 15 -

5. In paragraph 3, which words best convey the feelings of the doctors in Nome in 1925?
    a. "Epidemic" and "diphtheria"
    b. "Blizzards" and "windstorms"
    c. "Brave" and "frantic relay"
    d. "Desperate" and "cry for help"

6. Why did the author choose to write this article in third-person point of view?
    a. Historical overviews are best written in third person
    b. The author has never been to Alaska
    c. Third person is the required point of view in nonfiction writing
    d. This article is not written in third-person point of view

7. In what year did the Iditarod Trail become a National Historic Trail?
    a. 1967
    b. 1973
    c. 1978
    d. 1981

8. Which of the following is the best summary of the history of the Iditarod Trail race?
    a. After the Iditarod Trail became a National Historic Trail, the race became more popular, and today many mushers participate each year
    b. After a slow start in 1967, the Iditarod Trail race became firmly established in 1973, and it continues in popularity today
    c. In the first race in 1973, 34 mushers began the race, but only 22 were able to finish, proving that the race was just too hard
    d. Mushers between 14 and 18 years of age can race in the Junior Iditarod, while those over 18 can participate in the main race if they qualify

9. How is this article organized?
    a. Chronologically
    b. Geographically
    c. Randomly
    d. Spatially

10. Which of the following is a supporting detail in this article?
    a. Alaska's Iditarod Trail is the world's most famous sled dog racing venue
    b. After the heroic journey of 1925, mushing became more popular
    c. Some mushers run their dogs over 1,500 miles to prepare for the race
    d. There are specific requirements to enter the Iditarod Trail race

11. What do participants receive at the first mushers' banquet?
    a. Awards
    b. Racing order numbers
    c. Supplies
    d. Trail maps

12. What is the interval used to separate mushers as they begin the Iditarod Trail race?
    a. Five minutes
    b. One minute
    c. Ten minutes
    d. Two minutes

Questions 13 –24 pertain to the following story:

The Right Thing to Do

Characters *(in order of appearance)*:
JESSICA—a sixth-grade girl, Amy's friend
GROUP OF FRIENDS—a group of sixth-grade girls
AMY—a sixth-grade girl, Jessica's friend
SALES CLERK—a clerk in the store Amy and Jessica visit

Scene 1
(1) *Jessica stands with a group of friends on the school steps. The group is chatting and laughing. Amy approaches from stage right.*
(2) AMY: Jessica! Jessica!
(3) JESSICA: *(turning away from her friends and taking a step toward Amy)* Hi, Amy. What's up?
(4) AMY: I'm headed to the mall, and I thought you might want to come.
(5) JESSICA: Why me? I thought we weren't friends anymore.
(6) AMY: *(waving her hand and shaking her head)* That old fight? Ancient history. So … do you want to come or not?
(7) JESSICA: *(glancing back at her friends)* Sure. I'll come. Just give me a minute.
(8) *Jessica runs back and talks with her friends for a moment, then rejoins Amy. Amy and Jessica exit stage right.*
Scene 2
(9) *Amy and Jessica are looking at a shelf full of lipstick in a cosmetics store in the mall.*
(10) AMY: Look at this one, Jess. Don't you just love this color? *(She picks up a lipstick tube.)*
(11) JESSICA: It's nice, but I like this one better. *(She picks up a different tube of lipstick.)*
(12) *A sales clerk enters from stage left.*
(13) SALES CLERK: *(stopping by the girls)* Can I help you ladies find something?
(14) AMY: Oh, no. We're just looking.
(15) JESSICA: Thank you, though.
(16) SALES CLERK: Okay. Well, let me know if you need anything. *(He/she exits stage right.)*
(17) AMY: So, which one are you going to get?
(18) JESSICA: *(looking at the floor and shaking her head)* I'm not getting one. They're a little spendy for me. Besides, I'm saving up for something special.
(19) AMY: *(laughing)* Who said anything about money? *(She slips her favorite lipstick into her pocket.)* I didn't ask you which one you were going to buy. I asked which one you were going to get. So, which one will it be?
(20) JESSICA: But—but—that's stealing!

- 17 -

(21) AMY: Look at all these tubes of lipstick. They'll never miss a couple.

(22) JESSICA: *(looking around nervously)* What if that sales clerk comes back and catches us?

(23) AMY: You worry too much. *(She picks up two tubes of lipstick.)* Now, was this the one you liked? Or was it this one? Never mind. We'll take them both. *(She slips them both into her pocket.)*

(24) JESSICA: Amy! This is wrong. We shouldn't be doing this.

(25) AMY: *(glaring at Jessica)* Do you even want to be my friend again? It sure doesn't sound like it.

(26) JESSICA: Of course I want to be your friend. It's just—

(27) AMY: Then come on. Let's go. *(She starts to walk away, and then turns and looks back.)* Are you coming?

(28) JESSICA: Fine. *(She follows Amy.)* But what if the alarm goes off?

(29) AMY: For a couple of tubes of lipstick? Not gonna happen. Now, follow me. And for heaven's sake, don't look so nervous.

(30) *The girls exit stage right.*

Scene 3

(31) *Jessica reenters the cosmetics store from stage right. She stops at the shelf of lipsticks and looks around. The sales clerk enters from stage left.*

(32) JESSICA: Excuse me ...

(33) SALES CLERK: *(stopping)* Did you need help with something?

(34) JESSICA: Yes. *(She looks at the floor.)* My friend who was just with me, um, she took—well, actually, she stole three tubes of lipstick. I'm not okay with that. So, um, I wanted to pay for them.

(35) SALES CLERK: That's impressive. I've never seen that happen before. And kids take stuff from this store all the time. What made you come back?

(36) JESSICA: *(shrugging)* I don't know. I guess it was just the right thing to do.

13. In paragraph 6, what does Amy mean when she calls her fight with Jessica "ancient history"?
   a. It happened thousands of years ago
   b. It happened in history class
   c. Amy has totally forgotten about the fight
   d. They were arguing about events in ancient history

14. What is the setting for Scene 1?
   a. The school steps
   b. The mall
   c. A cosmetics store
   d. Amy's house

15. What is the setting for Scene 2 and Scene 3?
   a. The school steps
   b. Jessica's house
   c. A cosmetics store
   d. Amy's house

16. Which scene contains the climax of this play?
    a. Scene 1
    b. Scene 2
    c. Scene 3
    d. All of the above

17. Which scene contains the denouement of this play?
    a. Scene 1
    b. Scene 2
    c. Scene 3
    d. All of the above

18. In paragraph 29, why is the word "gonna" considered acceptable?
    a. It shows Amy's pattern of slang speech
    b. It is always acceptable in written English
    c. It is a different language spoken by Amy
    d. It is not acceptable; it is a misspelling

19. In paragraph 6, what type of figurative language is used when Amy says "ancient history"?
    a. Metaphor
    b. Simile
    c. Personification
    d. Hyperbole

20. Which of the following best describes the overall tone of this play?
    a. Formal
    b. Conversational
    c. Classical
    d. Musical

21. What is the underlying theme of this play?
    a. Amy and Jessica are best friends
    b. Doing the right thing is always a good decision
    c. It is okay to steal if you are not caught
    d. Shopping for cosmetics increases peer pressure

22. Which paragraph best shows Amy's justification for stealing the lipstick?
    a. Paragraph 21
    b. Paragraph 23
    c. Paragraph 25
    d. Paragraph 29

23. Why does Jessica say she is not buying lipstick?
    a. She does not wear lipstick
    b. She does not like any of the lipstick colors
    c. She wants Amy to buy a lipstick for her
    d. The lipstick is expensive, and she is saving her money

24. Which of the following is the best summary of this play?
   a. Jessica leaves her other friends to be friends with Amy again, and she and Amy go to the mall
   b. Amy teaches Jessica how to steal lipstick without getting caught, being a bad influence on Jessica
   c. Jessica agrees to go to the mall with Amy, but when Amy steals lipstick, Jessica goes back to pay for it
   d. Jessica thinks stealing is wrong, and she thinks Amy is a bad influence because she is a thief

Questions 25 – 36 pertain to the following two short stories:

The Talent Show

(1) The first notes floated from the piano. Megan smiled, warm and excited beneath the glaring stage lights. This was her moment. She had practiced. She had prepared. She was ready. As the introduction ended, Megan opened her mouth and began to sing.

(2) The song flowed along, and Megan relaxed, scanning the faces of the audience. But somewhere in the middle of the second verse, her mind suddenly went blank. The music went on, but the words were gone. Megan's smile faded. She stood silently with her mouth hanging open. When the music finally trickled to a stop, Megan ran from the stage.

(3) In a cramped dressing room backstage, Megan buried her face in her hands. She had wanted so much to win this talent show. Tears seeped between her fingers. Her confidence and pride and excitement had been replaced by utter disappointment. She felt a hand on her shoulder and lifted her damp face.

(4) "Ella and Kaylee are here," Megan's mom said, giving her shoulder a quick squeeze.

(5) Ella and Kaylee, Megan's two best friends, pulled folding chairs over to face Megan. She looked at them forlornly.

(6) "I'm a total failure," she moaned.

(7) Ella and Kaylee exchanged glances. Kaylee reached out and squeezed Megan's hand.

(8) "What are you talking about?" Kaylee said. "That first verse was some of your best singing ever."

(9) "Thanks," Megan said. "But the problem is that the first verse is all I sang. Then I totally bombed. I can't believe I forgot the words after all that practice."

(10) "You didn't totally bomb," Ella said. "You just forgot the words. That happens to everybody. Besides, don't the pros say you should leave your audience wanting more?"

(11) "I guess so," Megan admitted.

(12) "Well, trust me," Ella said. "I guarantee they wanted more—like the rest of the song! You probably did, too."

(13) Megan smiled a little. "So, you guys don't think I'm a total dork for forgetting the words?"

(14) "Of course not," Kaylee said. "Forgetting the words doesn't make you a dork. It just makes you human. And you're still the most talented person I know."

(15) Ella nodded in agreement. Megan pulled Ella and Kaylee into a quick hug. Then she wiped her eyes and managed a genuine smile.

(16) "I'm so lucky to have best friends like you two," Megan said. "It's nice to know that you'll be my friends forever, no matter what!"

The Tournament

(1) Looking for a hole in the defense, Scott dribbled the ball, shifting it from hand to hand. A trickle of sweat ran down his back. No one was open. There were only seconds left on the clock, and Scott knew he had a difficult decision to make.

(2) The other team was leading by two points, and Scott was just outside the three-point line. If he could make the shot, the Eagles would be state champions again. But if he missed ... Scott didn't want to think about that. He knew what he had to do.

(3) It was a classic jump shot. The ball left his hands and sailed toward the basket in a perfect arc. The crowd, the other players, the whole stadium seemed frozen in time. All eyes were on the ball as it struck the rim and bounced off. The buzzer blared. The game was over. Scott had missed, and the Eagles had lost.

(4) Scott stood like a statue on the court as people surged around him. Elated family members swarmed the winning team. Teammates hugged and slapped each other on the back. Even Scott's own teammates joined in the celebration.

(5) Suddenly, Scott felt himself being hoisted unsteadily onto the shoulders of his friends. Over the loudspeaker, the announcer proclaimed that Scott had been named the most valuable player of the championship game. Everyone cheered, and the Eagles took a victory lap with Scott on their shoulders. Finally, Scott's friends put him back on solid ground.

(6) Scott was bewildered. He was the one who missed the most important shot of the game. How could anyone call him the most valuable player? He didn't feel very valuable at the moment. Scott approached Coach Travis.

(7) "Coach," Scott said, "there must be some mistake. I can't be the most valuable player."

(8) "There's no mistake," Coach Travis said. "You had 26 points, 11 rebounds, and 8 assists. I'd say that makes you a very valuable player."

(9) "But I missed that last shot," Scott said. "We lost the game because of me."

(10) "I don't know about that," said Coach Travis. "Everybody misses a shot from time to time. Don't be so hard on yourself. It's all about perspective."

(11) "What do you mean?" Scott asked.

(12) "Well," Coach Travis answered, "you could say you are the reason we lost the game because you missed that last shot. On the other hand, you could say you are the reason we almost won because of your awesome performance throughout the game. How you look at it is up to you."

(13) Scott's teammates came running over and surrounded Coach Travis. They jostled one another playfully, talking and laughing.

(14) "Hey, Coach," one player called out, "how about treating your team to pizza?"

(15) "I don't know," said Coach Travis. "Do you think you deserve pizza?"

(16) Scott piped up. "Of course we do! After all, we almost won the game."
(17) Coach Travis smiled. "You're right, Scott. We did almost win. Okay. Pizza for everyone!"

Questions 25-29 pertain to "The Talent Show" short story.

25. Which of the following is the best definition of "forlornly" as it is used in paragraph 5?
    a. With a happy spirit
    b. With a sad spirit
    c. With a lonely spirit
    d. With an angry spirit

26. What is the main theme of this story?
    a. Real friends support you, no matter what
    b. It is easy to forget the words of a song
    c. Performing in a talent show can be embarrassing
    d. Megan feels like a failure

27. What point of view is used to tell this story?
    a. First person
    b. Second person
    c. Third person
    d. None of the above

28. Which of the following is a supporting detail in this story?
    a. Megan is singing in a talent show
    b. Megan forgets the words of her song
    c. Megan is disappointed in herself
    d. Megan is accompanied by piano music

29. What does Kaylee do in paragraph 8 to try to make Megan feel better?
    a. She makes a joke about Megan's performance
    b. She compliments Megan on her singing
    c. She tells about a time when she forgot a song
    d. She sings a song with Megan

Questions 30-34 pertain to "The Tournament" short story.

30. In paragraph 4, what does "elated" mean?
    a. Happy and excited
    b. Frustrated and angry
    c. Loud and rowdy
    d. Pushy and proud

31. In the first sentence of paragraph 4, what type of figurative language is used?
    a. Hyperbole
    b. Metaphor
    c. Personification
    d. Simile

- 22 -

32. Which of the following best expresses the theme of this story?
    a. The Eagles want to be the state champions
    b. There are different ways to look at any situation
    c. Winning isn't everything
    d. Scott is a very good basketball player

33. Which of the following is the best summary of this story?
    a. At the buzzer, Scott misses an important basket because he isn't a very good basketball player
    b. Coach Travis feels Scott is the most valuable player in the game because he scored 26 points
    c. When Scott misses an important shot, he is disappointed, but Coach Travis shows him there are different ways to look at the situation
    d. The Eagles lose the state championship because of Scott, but Coach Travis sees things differently and makes Scott the most valuable player

34. Why is Scott so upset in this story?
    a. He feels responsible for losing the game
    b. He thinks he is a bad basketball player
    c. He doesn't like Coach Travis
    d. He doesn't want to play basketball anymore

Questions 35-36 pertain to both "The Talent Show" and "The Tournament" short stories.

35. In what ways are Scott and Megan most similar in these stories?
    a. They are both performers.
    b. They are both very active.
    c. They are both disappointed in themselves.
    d. They both have good friends.

36. What general theme is evident in both stories?
    a. Winning is important, but it isn't everything
    b. Good friends are the most valuable thing in life
    c. Coaches can offer good perspective on tough situations
    d. When you try your best, you shouldn't be disappointed in yourself

Questions 37-48 pertain to the following story:

Everybody's Problem

(1) I used to think homeless people were dirty and lazy and mean. I thought they were all old men with scraggly beards and mangy dogs. I thought they lived on the street because they wanted to. I thought they were all drug addicts and alcoholics who ate from garbage cans and slept in boxes. I used to think homelessness wasn't my problem. Then I met Chris, and he showed me I was wrong—about everything. Homelessness is everybody's problem.
(2) The sun was climbing into the bright blue sky as we loaded up the bus at the youth center. It was a crisp, cold Thanksgiving morning, and our youth group was headed down to a local shelter called The Lighthouse. We were going to serve Thanksgiving dinner to more than a hundred homeless people. It seemed like an appropriate way to spend Thanksgiving Day.

- 23 -

(3) When we arrived at the shelter, we were each given a job to do. My job was peeling potatoes. The shelter director gave me a peeler and a garbage can and sat me down in front of a giant pile of potatoes. I had never seen so many potatoes in one place before. They rose from the tray like Mt. Everest. By the time I had peeled them all, my hands and arms and shoulders ached.

(4) When the kitchen work was done, we were given our serving stations. The director explained that this was the only meal many of the homeless people would eat that day, and for some, it was the only hot meal they would have that week. Even so, there wasn't a lot of food for so many people. We were supposed to give each person one slice of turkey, one scoop of mashed potatoes, one scoop of stuffing, a small drizzle of gravy, a few green beans, and a sliver of pumpkin pie.

(5) I was plodding along, dishing up mashed potatoes with an ice cream scoop, when I happened to look up at the person I was serving. He wasn't a dirty, bearded old man. He was a boy about my age, with brown hair and brown eyes and a patched green jacket.

(6) "Hi," the boy said. "I'm Chris."

(7) "I'm Ben," I said as I scooped some potatoes onto his plate. "Happy Thanksgiving."

(8) "Thanks," Chris said, and then he was gone.

(9) As Chris moved down the line, I began to look around, really seeing things for the first time. Very few of the homeless people fit my stereotype. There were men and women, old and young. Children played in a corner of the dining room. At one table, teenagers talked in a tight group. People chatted and smiled. A few were even laughing. This was not what I had pictured a homeless shelter would be like.

(10) When everyone had been served, I began to help clean up. I couldn't help watching Chris as I cleared the tables and wiped them down. He was playing peek-a-boo with a little girl in a high chair. I wondered if it was his little sister.

(11) I was so lost in thought that I jumped when the shelter director tapped my shoulder. She laughed.

(12) "I'll finish cleaning up here," she said. "Why don't you go talk to Chris? He's very nice."

(13) As I approached the table where Chris was sitting, I felt nervous. What would I say? Could we possibly have anything to talk about? Would he even want to talk to me? I sat cautiously beside him.

(14) "Hi, Ben," he said.

(15) "Hi, Chris. Is that your little sister?"

(16) Chris smiled. "Yep. This is Sophia. And over there is my little brother, Dane." Chris motioned toward the corner where the smaller children were playing. Then he pointed to a dark-haired woman at a nearby table. "That's my mom."

(17) "Are you all homeless?" I asked.

(18) "Yep," answered Chris. "We've been here at The Lighthouse for almost two months now. It's okay here, but I miss my old school and my friends. I hope we can move back to a real house soon."

(19) "I didn't know there was such a thing as homeless kids," I admitted.

(20) "Me neither," said Chris. "At least, not until I became one."

(21) "How did it happen?" I asked. Then I had second thoughts. "I mean, you don't have to tell me if you don't want to. I was just wondering."

(22) "It's okay," Chris said. "I don't mind talking about it. About a year ago, my dad got really sick. He was in the hospital for a few months. Then he died. We didn't have any insurance or anything, and my mom couldn't get a job. Besides, she was really sad, and she was trying to take care of me and Dane and Sophia."

(23) "So, how did you end up homeless?" I wondered.

(24) "Mom says there were just too many bills and not enough money. First, we got our lights turned off. Then we couldn't pay our rent, so we had to move out of our house. We stayed with friends for a while, but eventually there was nobody left to stay with. So, we came here."

(25) "Will you stay here forever?" I asked.

(26) "No," Chris said. "My mom is in a program to give her training and help her get a job. When she finds a job, we can get a new place to live. Then things can be normal again."

(27) I heard my youth leader calling for us to load the bus. I wanted to talk to Chris more and ask him more questions, but I knew I had to leave. I stood up.

(28) "I have to go," I said. "I'm glad I got to meet you, Chris. I hope you get a new house soon."

(29) "Thanks, Ben," Chris said. "It was nice to meet you, too. Thanks for hanging out with me for a while. Happy Thanksgiving."

(30) "Happy Thanksgiving," I echoed as I headed toward the door. When I looked back, Chris waved. Then he started playing peek-a-boo with Sophia again.

(31) I will probably never see Chris again, but I have thought of him many times since that day. In just a few minutes together, he taught me so much about the problem of homelessness. It isn't just a problem that affects lazy, mean old men. It affects men and women of all ages. It affects children. It affects whole families. It affected Chris. And because I got the chance to see homelessness through his eyes, it affects me now, too. I think I'll go back again next Thanksgiving ... or maybe sooner. After all, now I know that homelessness is everybody's problem.

37. What is the setting for this story?
    a. A youth center
    b. A homeless shelter
    c. A community center
    d. A school

38. If you were describing this story, what classification would you use?
    a. Memoir
    b. Biography
    c. Autobiography
    d. Fiction

39. In paragraph 9, what does the word "stereotype" mean?
    a. A textbook definition of a concept
    b. Height, weight, and physical features
    c. A generalized idea of what something is like
    d. A description given by an authority figure

40. What point of view is used to tell this story?
    a. First person
    b. Second person
    c. Third person
    d. All of the above

41. What is the main theme of this story?
    a. Kids can be homeless
    b. Potatoes are difficult to peel
    c. Serving at a homeless shelter is a good Thanksgiving project
    d. Homelessness is everybody's problem

42. What does the author compare the potatoes to in paragraph 3?
    a. A tower
    b. A mountain range
    c. Mt. Everest
    d. A mound

43. Which of the following items was not included in the Thanksgiving dinner at the shelter?
    a. Turkey
    b. Cranberry sauce
    c. Mashed potatoes and gravy
    d. Pumpkin pie

44. What major event in the life of Chris's family led to their homelessness?
    a. Their house burned down
    b. Chris's mom lost her job
    c. They had to live in their car
    d. Chris's dad got sick and died

45. How does meeting Chris change Ben's mind about homelessness?
    a. It doesn't change Ben's mind at all
    b. It makes Ben afraid of being homeless
    c. It helps Ben see that homelessness affects everyone
    d. It keeps Ben from ever helping in a homeless shelter again

46. What do you think the author's primary purpose was in telling this story?
    a. To persuade the reader to do something about homelessness
    b. To inform the reader about The Lighthouse homeless shelter
    c. To educate the reader on Thanksgiving service projects
    d. To entertain the reader with a story about a personal experience

47. Which of the following is the best summary of this story?
   a. In the beginning, Ben hates homeless people, but at the end, he loves them
   b. Ben goes to a homeless shelter to serve Thanksgiving dinner and learns that homelessness affects everyone
   c. The Lighthouse is a wonderful shelter that serves individuals and families who are homeless
   d. Ben peels potatoes, serves food, meets Chris, and then goes home

48. Which of the following is Ben most likely to do in the future as a result of meeting Chris at The Lighthouse?
   a. Avoid homeless people
   b. Give away all his money
   c. Try living on the street
   d. Serve at a homeless shelter again

Answers and Explanations

1. B: is the best choice because the simile in paragraph 1—"like a mirage"—refers to the path. A, C, and D are not the best choices because they are not the subjects of the simile.

2. C: is the best choice because "landlocked" means "not on a waterway." A, B, and D are not the best choices because they offer incorrect definitions of "landlocked."

3. A: is the best choice because Anchorage and Nome are at the ends of the Iditarod Trail. B, C, and D are not the best choices because they are not the two cities at the ends of the Iditarod Trail.

4. D: is the best choice because the author's main purpose in writing this article is to educate the reader about the Iditarod Trail. A, B, and C are not the best choices because they do not accurately represent the author's main purpose in writing this article.

5. D: is the best choice because "desperate" and "cry for help" are the words that best represent the feelings of the doctors in Nome in 1925. A, B, and C are not the best choices because they do not reflect the feelings of the doctors.

6. A: is the best choice because historical overviews, like this one, are best written in third-person point of view. B and C are not the best choices because they are not valid reasons for writing in third person. D is not the best choice because the article is written in third-person point of view.

7. C: is the best choice because the Iditarod Trail became a National Historic Trail in 1978. A, B, and D are not the best choices because they do not accurately represent the year the Iditarod Trail became a National Historic Trail.

8. B: is the best choice because it offers the most accurate summary of the history of the Iditarod Trail race. A, C, and D are not the best choices because they are not accurate and complete summaries of the history of the Iditarod Trail as presented in the article.

9. A: is the best choice because this article is organized chronologically, from earliest to latest dates. B, C, and D are not the best choices because the article is not organized geographically, randomly, or spatially.

10. C: is the best choice because it is a supporting detail that expands on a main idea from the article. A, B, and D are not the best choices because they are all main ideas in the article instead of supporting details.

11. B: is the best choice because at the first mushers' banquet the race participants receive their racing order numbers. A, C, and D are not the best choices because they are not things received by participants at the first mushers' banquet.

12. D: is the best choice because as they begin the Iditarod Trail race, mushers are separated by two-minute intervals. A, B, and C are not the best choices because mushers are not separated by five-minute, one-minute, or ten-minute intervals.

13. C: is the best choice because the phrase "ancient history" is used to communicate that Amy has totally forgotten about the fight. A, B, and D are not the best choices because the play does not indicate that the fight was related to history or history class, and it clearly did not occur thousands of years ago.

14. A: is the best choice because Scene 1 is set on the school steps. B, C, and D are not the best choices because they do not accurately represent the setting of Scene 1.

15. D: is the best choice because Scene 2 and Scene 3 take place in a cosmetics store. A, B, and C are not the best choices because they do not accurately represent the setting of Scene 2 and Scene 3.

16. B: is the best choice because Scene 2 contains the climax of the play, when Jessica must decide whether to go along with Amy or not. A, C, and D are not the best choices because they do not reflect the scene that contains the climax of the play.

17. C: is the best choice because Scene 3 contains the denouement of the play, when Jessica returns to the store to do the right thing. A, B, and D are not the best choices because they do not reflect the scene that contains the denouement.

18. A: is the best choice because the word "gonna" is used to show Amy's slang speech pattern. B and C are not the best choices because they are not true statements. D is not the best choice because in this context, the word "gonna" is acceptable and is not a misspelling.

19. D: is the best choice because the use of "ancient history" in paragraph 6 is a hyperbole, a major exaggeration. A, B, and C are not the best choices because "ancient history" is not an example of metaphor, simile, or personification.

20. B: is the best choice because the overall tone of this play is conversational. A, C, and D are not the best choices because the tone of the play is not formal, classical, or musical.

21. B: is the best choice because it best represents the underlying theme of the play. A, C, and D are not the best choices because they do not accurately represent the underlying theme of the play.

22. A: is the best choice because paragraph 21 best shows Amy's justification for stealing the lipsticks. B, C, and D are not the best choices because they do not clearly reflect Amy's justification for stealing the lipsticks.

23. D: is the best choice because it truly reflects the reason Jessica gives in the play for not buying lipstick. A, B, and C are not the best choices because they do not accurately represent the reason Jessica gave for not buying lipstick.

24. C: is the best choice because it is the most accurate and complete summary of the play. A, B, and D are not the best choices because they do not offer complete and accurate summaries of the play.

25. B: is the best choice because "forlornly" is best defined as "with a sad spirit." A, C, and D are not the best choices because they are not proper definitions of the word "forlornly."

26. A: is the best choice because it most accurately represents the main theme of the story. B, C, and D are not the best choices because they do not represent true themes of this story.

27. C: is the best choice because this story is written in third person. A and B are not the best choices, because the story is not written in first or second person. D is not the best choice because the story is written in third person.

28. D: is the best choice because it is the only option that offers a supporting detail rather than a main idea from the story. A, B, and C are not the best choices because they represent main ideas in the story, not supporting details.

29. B: is the best choice because in paragraph 8, Kaylee compliments Megan's singing to help Megan feel better. A, C, and D are not the best choices because they do not represent actions Kaylee took in paragraph 8 to help Megan feel better.

30. A: is the best choice because it is the best definition of "elated." B, C, and D are not the best choices because they are not correct definitions of the word "elated."

31. D: is the best choice because the first sentence of paragraph 4 uses a simile to compare Scott to a statue. A, B, and C are not the best choices because the first sentence of paragraph 4 does not use hyperbole, metaphor, or personification.

32. B: is the best choice because it clearly and completely expresses the theme of the story. A, C, and D are not the best choices because they do not accurately reflect the main theme of the story.

33. C: is the best choice because it is the most complete and accurate summary of the story overall. A, B, and D are not the best choices because they cover only part of the story or some of the main ideas and concepts.

34. A: is the best choice: Scott is upset in the story because he feels responsible for the team's loss. B, C, and D are not the best choices because they do not represent true reasons Scott is upset in this story.

35. C: is the best choice because Scott and Megan are most similar in their feelings of disappointment in themselves. A, B, and D are not the best choices because they do not reflect strong similarities between Scott and Megan, as reflected in these two stories.

36. D: is the best choice because it clearly reflects a general theme found in both stories. A, B, and C are not the best choices because they do not represent general themes found in both stories.

37. B: is the best choice because this story is set at a homeless shelter. A, C, and D are not the best choices because they do not represent the correct setting of the story.

38. A: is the best choice because this story is written in the style of a memoir, as evidenced by the first-person, reflective tone. B, C, and D are not the best choices because this story is not written as a biography, autobiography, or fiction piece.

39. C: is the best choice because it offers the best definition of "stereotype" as it is used in paragraph 9. A, B, and D are not the best choices because they are not accurate definitions of "stereotype" as it is used in this story.

40. A: is the best choice because this story is written in first person. B and C are not the best choices because this story is not written in second or third person. D is not the best choice because this story is written from a single point of view.

41. D: is the best choice because the main theme of the story is that homelessness is everybody's problem. A, B, and C are not the best choices because they do not accurately represent the theme of this story.

42. C: is the best choice because in paragraph 3 the potatoes are compared to Mt. Everest. A, B, and D are not the best choices because the potatoes are not compared to a tower, a mountain range, or a mound in paragraph 3.

43. B: is the best choice because cranberry sauce was not served as part of the Thanksgiving dinner at the shelter. A, C, and D are not the best choices because turkey, mashed potatoes and gravy, and pumpkin pie were all served at the Thanksgiving dinner at the shelter.

44. D: is the best choice because the death of Chris's dad led to the family's homelessness. A, B, and C are not the best choices because they do not accurately reflect major life events that led to Chris's family's homelessness.

45. C: is the best choice because it best outlines Ben's change of attitude after he meets Chris. A, B, and D are not the best choices because they do not clearly represent the change in Ben's attitude after meeting Chris.

46. A: is the best choice because the author's intention in writing this piece is clearly to persuade the reader to do something about homelessness. B, C, and D are not the best choices because the author's intention is not to merely inform, educate, or entertain the reader.

47. B: is the best choice because it is the most complete and accurate summary of the story. A, C, and D are not the best choices because while they discuss elements of the story, they do not offer a complete and accurate summary.

48. D: is the best choice because the last paragraph of the story indicates that Ben is likely to serve at a homeless shelter again soon. A, B, and C are not the best choices because they do not represent likely actions for Ben based on the content of the story.

Practice Test #2

Practice Questions

Questions 1 – 12 pertain to the following article:

The Trouble with Tests

(1) Lisa was a good student. She studied hard, diligently did her homework, and turned in assignments on time. Whenever she had to take a test, however, Lisa had a problem. Her hands began to sweat and her stomach began to churn. She felt dizzy and breathless and sick. As a result, Lisa couldn't focus and always did poorly on tests. Her grades suffered, and so did her confidence level.

(2) Lisa's problem is a common one. Often called test anxiety, it includes any unusual stress symptoms that occur during tests. Symptoms can be as mild as light nausea or headache, or as severe as vomiting or uncontrollable shaking. Millions of students deal with test anxiety every year, but few realize it can be improved through three simple steps.

(3) The first step to improving test anxiety is better study habits. Proper preparation is an important step to overcoming test anxiety. It is important to develop regular study times, avoiding last minute "cramming" for a test. Studying heavily on the day of or night before a test can actually increase test anxiety in most students. The better option is to devote at least a half-hour block of time to reviewing class materials each day. This can help embed information in the brain, making it more accessible at test time.

(4) Using memory games and tools is another way to improve study habits. Using these tools and games can help students better retain information. It also makes learning more fun, reducing stress levels. Flashcards with key points or ideas can be very helpful when used alone or with a study partner. Mnemonic devices—silly sayings to help students recall complex concepts—are also helpful tools for reducing stress and improving test performance. An example of a mnemonic device is "Every Good Boy Deserves Fudge" to help music students remember the note names for the lines of the treble clef staff (EGBDF).

(5) The second step to reducing test anxiety is to use relaxation techniques. The first relaxation technique that is useful for test anxiety is visualization. This involves choosing a favorite place or event. When test anxiety symptoms appear, students can close their eyes and visualize themselves in that favorite place or at that favorite event. The students should focus on sensory information—sights, sounds, smells, etc. This refocuses the attention of the brain and reduces anxiety.

(6) Another relaxation technique that works well for test anxiety is deep breathing. When the body is under stress, breathing becomes shallower, causing the heart rate to increase and the blood pressure to rise. Conscious deep breathing helps increase oxygen flow to the body, reducing the heart rate and blood pressure. To do deep breathing, simply draw air in through the nose for five seconds, and then release the air through the mouth,

blowing out steadily for five seconds. Done with eyes open or closed, deep breathing exercises reduce stress and relax the body.

(7) The third step to reducing test anxiety is positive self-talk. Often, test anxiety is the result of or is compounded by a lack of faith in abilities. Students can overcome this through positive self-talk and self-affirmation. Before each test, a student should repeat, "I can do this"—or some similar positive mantra—over and over. This can be done out loud or silently; either way, it creates a positive attitude and outlook that can reduce anxiety.

(8) The self-affirmation of celebrating success is a final key to overcoming test anxiety. Students should share test-taking victories with friends and loved ones. Students should also feel proud when they do well on a test. Every success is a blow to the obstacle of test anxiety. As with anything else, practice makes perfect, and celebrating success helps a student practice triumph over test anxiety.

(9) Test anxiety is a real problem, not an imagined issue or an excuse. It can be overcome, however, through three basic steps. First, students must use study tools and good habits for proper preparation. Second, students must use relaxation techniques—such as visualization and deep breathing—to help release stress from the body. Finally, students must engage in positive self-talk and celebrate successes to create an atmosphere of triumph. When all three of these steps are consistently practiced, test anxiety will become a thing of the past.

1. According to this article, what is test anxiety?
    a. A hereditary psychological disease
    b. Unusual stress symptoms that occur during tests
    c. An allergy to stress that is triggered by tests
    d. Headaches and nausea that occur after tests

2. What is a mnemonic device?
    a. A silly saying used to help remember a complex concept
    b. A tool that increases physical relaxation during a test
    c. An old-fashioned torture device involving repeated testing
    d. A tool for selecting answers on tests

3. What is the main purpose of this article?
    a. To show that test anxiety is a common problem
    b. To discuss Lisa's problems with test anxiety
    c. To identify the symptoms of test anxiety
    d. To identify potential solutions for test anxiety

4. What is the general tone of this article?
    a. Entertaining
    b. Persuasive
    c. Informative
    d. Fictional

5. Which of the following offers the best summary of this article?
  a. Test anxiety is a common problem that can be improved through three simple steps
  b. Lisa has test anxiety, and she needs to learn how to deal with it better
  c. Relaxation techniques are the best method for preventing test anxiety
  d. Good study habits are the best tools for preventing test anxiety

6. According to paragraph 3, what common study practice should be avoided?
  a. Using flashcards
  b. Studying with a partner
  c. Last-minute studying
  d. Overstudying

7. What is the first step to improving test anxiety?
  a. Better study habits
  b. Relaxation techniques
  c. Self-affirmation and positive self-talk
  d. Teamwork and study partners

8. What is the third step to reducing test anxiety?
  a. Better study habits
  b. Positive self-talk
  c. Visualization
  d. Relaxation techniques

9. Which of the following ideas is a supporting detail in this article?
  a. Millions of students deal with test anxiety every year
  b. Using memory games and tools improves study habits
  c. Test anxiety is a real problem
  d. "Every Good Boy Deserves Fudge" is an example of a study tool

10. What organizational pattern is used for this article?
  a. Inverted pyramid
  b. Proposition and support
  c. Problem and solution
  d. Simple exposition

11. What two specific relaxation techniques are discussed in this article?
  a. Massage and deep breathing
  b. Visualization and muscle tensing
  c. Meditation and massage
  d. Visualization and deep breathing

12. Which paragraph discusses the "final key" to overcoming test anxiety?
  a. Paragraph 6
  b. Paragraph 8
  c. Paragraph 7
  d. Paragraph 9

- 34 -

Questions 13-17 pertain to the following poem:

Fog

       (1) Stealthy fog drifts through the air,
       (2) A dense, gray blanket everywhere.
       (3) It slowly seeps in from the sea,
       (4) Clutching rooftops, climbing trees.

       (5) Its eerie whisper fills the land—
       (6) "Catch me, catch me, if you can!"
       (7) It skims the sky and hugs the ground,
       (8) Distorts the vision, muffles sound.

       (9) It fills the mind and fools the feet
       (10) Like haunting shadows in the street.
       (11) It creeps across the alleyway
       (12) And dims the newborn light of day.

       (13) It smothers landscapes without shame
       (14) Then fades as quickly as it came.

13. Which of the following is the best synonym for "stealthy"?
    a. Evil
    b. Careful
    c. Sneaky
    d. Thick

14. What type of figurative language is used in line 5?
    a. Personification
    b. Metaphor
    c. Simile
    d. Hyperbole

15. What does the poet accomplish by using figurative language throughout this poem?
    a. The poet meets the basic requirements of poetry
    b. The poet makes the fog seem alive
    c. The poet confuses and overwhelms the reader
    d. The poet gives additional length to the poem

16. To what is the fog compared in line 2?
    a. A whisper
    b. The sea
    c. A shadow
    d. A blanket

17. Which of the following best describes the rhyming pattern of this poem?
    a. ABAB CDCD EFEF GG
    b. AAAA BBBB CCCC DD
    c. ABCD EFGH IJKL MN
    d. AABB CCDD EEFF GG

- 35 -

Questions 18 – 22 pertain to the following poem:

Summer Afternoon

(1) Golden sunlight bathes the meadow
(2) In brilliant midday glory.
(3) Slim green pillars bow in homage
(4) To a gentle summer breeze.
(5) Flowers turn their eager faces
(6) Upward to an azure sky.
(7) All is quiet, calm, and peaceful,
(8) Dozing in the pleasant heat.

(9) Just across the sleepy meadow
(10) A lazy stream meanders through,
(11) Sauntering between the banks
(12) Of hardened, sun-baked earth.
(13) Dragonflies flit to and fro
(14) Like scattered thoughts and fleeting dreams.
(15) Bright light glistens on the water
(16) Like sparkling, molten silver.

(17) The meadow rests in tacit glow
(18) As minutes turn to hours.
(19) The sun sinks lower in the sky,
(20) And shadows slowly lengthen.
(21) Daylight, dappled by the trees,
(22) Spreads across the open landscape
(23) Like a dim and dusky cloak,
(24) And—in silence—evening falls.

18. What do lines 3 and 4 refer to in a metaphor?
    a. Green buildings in the field
    b. Grasses waving in the wind
    c. Trees waving in the wind
    d. People worshipping the wind

19. What type of figurative language is used in lines 13 and 14?
    a. Simile
    b. Metaphor
    c. Hyperbole
    d. Personification

20. What does "tacit" mean in line 17?
    a. Beautiful
    b. Lazy
    c. Silent
    d. Bored

21. Which of the following best describes the mood of this poem?
    a. Upbeat and exciting
    b. Quiet and peaceful
    c. Depressing and sullen
    d. Happy and energetic

22. How many stanzas does this poem contain?
    a. 1
    b. 8
    c. 3
    d. 24

Questions 23 -24 pertain to both "Fog" and "Summer Afternoon":
23. What general theme is represented in both of these poems?
    a. Nature
    b. Water
    c. Emotions
    d. Time

24. What is the most important difference in the style of these two poems?
    a. One uses figurative language and the other does not
    b. One is longer than the other
    c. One is set at night and the other is set in the daytime
    d. One is rhymed and the other is free verse

Questions 25 – 36 pertain to the following story:

The Memory Quilt

(1) Kevin had been saving his allowance for months to buy a new bike. Now he was within a few dollars of his goal, and Grandma Ruth had offered to pay him to clean out her attic. Kevin was excited. The new bike was practically his!

(2) Early Saturday morning, Kevin's mom dropped him off at Grandma Ruth's house. Grandma Ruth hugged him. Then she walked upstairs with him and pointed him to a narrow ladder that led up to the attic.

(3) "It's a mess up there," she warned. "If you have any questions about anything, just ask. Most of it is old junk, though. You can sort things I won't want to keep into two piles—one to throw away and the other to donate to charity."

(4) Kevin climbed the ladder and looked around. Boxes and piles of old pictures and records and clothes littered the floor. It was a big job. He picked up a painting of flowers in a chipped wooden frame. It didn't look important, but Kevin thought he should check.

(5) "Grandma Ruth," he called, climbing down the ladder with the picture. "Is this important?"

(6) Grandma Ruth came out of her room and chuckled. "No, Kevin. Your grandfather and I bought that old picture at a yard sale years ago. Put it in the pile to donate to charity."

(7) Kevin climbed back up the ladder. He put the picture on the floor to start a pile for charity. Then he picked up an old, rusty toolbox. Like the old

- 37 -

picture, it didn't look important, but Kevin thought he should check, just to make sure.

(8) "Grandma Ruth," he called again, climbing down the ladder with the toolbox. "Is this important?"

(9) Grandma Ruth laughed gently. "No, Kevin. Your grandfather bought that toolbox when we bought this old house. He was quite the handyman. But I have no use for it now. Put it in the pile to donate. And Kevin?"

(10) "Yes, Grandma Ruth?"

(11) "You don't have to check with me about each thing. If it looks old and unused, you can donate it or throw it away. I trust your judgment. But you can still ask if you have any questions." She winked at Kevin and went back into her room.

(12) Kevin climbed back up the ladder. He sorted through the piles quickly. By lunchtime, he was almost halfway done. He climbed down and ate tuna fish sandwiches with Grandma Ruth in the dining room. After lunch, she gave him some boxes to take up to the attic. She told him to box up and carry down the items to be donated to charity.

(13) Kevin made his way awkwardly back to the attic, carrying the boxes. He packed things up and sorted through piles until just before 4 pm, when his mom was coming to pick him up. The last item he grabbed was a faded, dusty quilt. He turned it over and studied it carefully. It was worn, and it seemed like it hadn't been used in a long time. Kevin threw it into a charity box and closed the top. Then he began carrying boxes down the ladder.

(14) Kevin's mom drove him by the Goodwill store on the way home. Together they unloaded the boxes of items to be donated. Then they headed home, where Kevin fell asleep right after dinner. He was exhausted from his hard work.

(15) Sunday afternoon, Kevin went back to Grandma Ruth's house to finish cleaning out the attic. The piles were sparser now, but they still popped up from the dusty floor like wayward molehills. He got right to work, sorting, boxing things up, and neatly stacking the items to be kept.

(16) Halfway through the afternoon, Grandma Ruth called Kevin down for cookies and milk.

(17) "Kevin, have you seen my old patchwork quilt up in the attic?" Grandma Ruth asked. "I can't seem to find it anywhere. I made that quilt from your grandfather's old work shirts and your mom's first baby blanket and the tablecloth I got at my wedding. There are so many memories in that quilt."

(18) Kevin gulped. He didn't want to lie to Grandma Ruth, but he couldn't tell her he donated her precious quilt to charity. She would kill him!

(19) "I'll look for it when I go back up," he promised, knowing it wasn't there.

(20) At the end of the afternoon, Kevin was done cleaning the attic. He carried the last box down the ladder.

(21) "Did you see my quilt up there?" Grandma Ruth asked.

(22) "No," Kevin said, half-truthfully.

(23) "I wonder where it could be," Grandma Ruth said.

(24) When Kevin and his mom stopped at the Goodwill store to donate the last set of boxes, Kevin asked if he could run inside. He dashed in and browsed the shelves carefully. Then he saw it. It was stuffed between two stacks of throw pillows. It was almost hidden, but unmistakable. He pulled out the quilt and checked the price.

(25) Kevin's heart fell. Paying for the quilt would mean he would have to wait another month or two to buy his bike. If he just went home, no one would ever know about his mistake. But he knew that would be wrong. Buying the quilt back was the right thing to do. Kevin paid for the quilt and hurried back to the car.

(26) Kevin's mom looked at the quilt with surprise. "Isn't that Grandma Ruth's memory quilt?"

(27) Kevin nodded glumly. He told his mom the whole story. Then he said he needed to go back to Grandma Ruth's house to tell her the truth.

(28) "I'm proud of you," Kevin's mom said as she turned the car around. "Let's go give Grandma Ruth back her memories."

25. Which of the following is the best definition of "littered" as it is used in paragraph 4?
    a. Stacked neatly on
    b. Scattered across
    c. Piled on
    d. Put in a few places

26. What is the primary setting for this story?
    a. Grandma Ruth's attic
    b. The Goodwill store
    c. Kevin's house
    d. Grandma Ruth's dining room

27. In paragraph 15, what does "sparser" mean?
    a. Denser
    b. Larger and higher
    c. Fewer and smaller
    d. More organized

28. What point of view is used to tell this story?
    a. First person
    b. Second person
    c. Third person
    d. All of the above

29. What type of figurative language is used in paragraph 15?
    a. Metaphor
    b. Personification
    c. Hyperbole
    d. Simile

30. What is the general theme of this story?
    a. Help your grandmother
    b. Cleaning is best done in an organized way
    c. Do the right thing
    d. Never throw away or donate old items

31. Which paragraph contains the climax of this story?
    a. Paragraph 12
    b. Paragraph 16
    c. Paragraph 24
    d. Paragraph 25

32. Why was the quilt so valuable to Grandma Ruth?
    a. It contained fabric from memorable things
    b. It was sewn by hand by her grandmother
    c. She had used the quilt for many years
    d. It was a wedding present from Kevin's grandfather

33. Which of the following is a supporting detail in this story?
    a. Kevin was saving his allowance for a new bike
    b. Kevin and Grandma Ruth ate tuna fish sandwiches
    c. Kevin was cleaning out Grandma Ruth's attic
    d. Kevin donated Grandma Ruth's quilt to charity

34. Which of the following is the best summary of this story?
    a. Kevin spends his Saturday cleaning out Grandma Ruth's attic so he can buy a bike
    b. While cleaning out Grandma Ruth's attic, Kevin donates an important quilt to charity and has to get it back
    c. Grandma Ruth describes her memory quilt to Kevin while eating cookies and milk
    d. Kevin and his mom take Grandma Ruth's memory quilt back to her after finding it and buying it at Goodwill

35. Which of the following elements was not part of the memory quilt?
    a. Grandma Ruth's wedding dress
    b. Grandfather's old work shirts
    c. Kevin's mom's baby blanket
    d. Grandma Ruth's tablecloth

36. What type of figurative language is used at the end of paragraph 18?
    a. Simile
    b. Metaphor
    c. Personification
    d. Hyperbole

Questions 37 – 48 pertain to the following article:

Like Riding a Kite

(1) Imagine soaring high above the earth. There is no engine, no fuselage beneath you. There is only you, your glider, the wind, and the sky. It's like riding a kite with no strings attached, rising and falling on the breeze like a bird. It is freedom and thrill and ultimate pleasure. This is the world of hang gliding.

(2) While many people have a general idea of what hang gliding is all about, few really understand the sport. Most people don't realize a majestic glider can be collapsed to the size of a duffel bag. Few people know that gliders can stay aloft for hours and that the world distance record for a single glider

flight is nearly 190 miles. Even fewer people realize that a hang glider can actually climb in the sky, even without an engine. In California, in the 1980s, one expert glider pilot gained more than 14,000 feet of altitude after takeoff! Hang gliders have mind-boggling capabilities.

(3) The amazing sport of hang gliding has a rich history dating back to the 1890s. In 1891, the first hang glider was invented by Otto Lilienthal in Germany. It was made of wood and cloth, weighed 40 pounds, was 23 feet wide, and could go about 35 miles per hour (mph) at an altitude of 100 feet. British inventor Percy Picher also built gliders with similar features in the late 1890s. Unfortunately, both inventors were killed in glider crashes before their designs were perfected. With the element of danger involved in early hang gliding—and with the advent of airplane flight by the Wright brothers in 1903—many people lost interest in hang gliding.

(4) After the end of World War II, however, many military-trained pilots wanted to keep flying. Airplanes were too expensive for most people, so the sport of hang gliding was reborn. Through invention and innovation, new designs for hang gliders began to emerge. These included new materials and designs for glider construction and the addition of a control bar to improve safety. The basic design for today's hang gliders premiered at a meet in California in 1971. It included a broad, flexible wing on a sturdy frame with a control bar and a seat or safety harness.

(5) Since 1971, few major design changes have been made to hang gliders, although as new materials for construction become available, minor changes are made to improve flight. Modern sails range from 13 to 28 feet across. They are made of durable, lightweight, manmade fabric—such as nylon— and are designed to flex in shape and tension based on the wind. The sail is attached to a frame made from aluminum tubing. The frame includes a control bar, shaped like a rounded triangle and used for steering. Suspended from the frame is a harness or seat to improve pilot comfort and safety.

(6) Another way pilots improve comfort and safety is through the use of proper gear and equipment. Pilots should wear light, protective clothing and gloves designed for hang gliding. A helmet is also an important safety component. In addition, pilots need special instruments that are used during flight. These tools help measure thermals, the warm air currents used to lift and propel gliders through the air.

(7) Thermals are important to both taking off and staying aloft, but they aren't the only factor in flight. Modern gliders weigh about 35 pounds and are special balanced to a pilot's weight and preferences. To take off, the pilot is secured in the glider and then runs off the edge of a large hill or cliff, where thermals catch the glider and lift it into the air. If the wind is sustained above 12 mph, the pilot may even be able to take off without running. Once the glider is airborne, the pilot steers by shifting his/her weight and using the control bar. Each glider has its own unique feel, and a pilot must know the glider well to achieve a safe takeoff, flight, and landing.

(8) In addition to knowing the unique feel of the glider, a pilot must know the safety rules of the sky to have a safe flight. Pilots of hang gliders do not need to be licensed, but they must obey all rules and laws for flying. Hang glider pilots should never fly in bad weather or high winds. They must yield the right of way to any aircraft in distress and all hot air balloons. They must never intentionally fly into a cloud or a flock of birds. Finally, hang glider

pilots should stay at least five miles away from airports during flight and at least 100 feet from buildings, telephone wires and poles, populated places, and crowds.

(9) Throughout history, mankind has looked for a way to soar with the birds across the canvas of the sky. Hang gliding offers that opportunity. With modern features and equipment, and with proper training in techniques and the rules of the sky, hang glider pilots can safely experience the thrill of flight. In a glider, the pilot is one with the breeze, the sunlight, the world itself. Hang gliding is truly like riding a kite through the expanse of the heavens.

37. In paragraph 3, what does "advent" mean?
   a. End
   b. Beginning
   c. Expansion
   d. Popularity

38. Which of the following is the best definition of "thermals" as it is used in this article?
   a. Protective clothing for pilots
   b. Aluminum tubing used in glider frames
   c. Tools used by pilots for safety
   d. Warm air currents that lift gliders

39. What was the author's main purpose in writing this article?
   a. To inform
   b. To entertain
   c. To analyze
   d. To persuade

40. What type of figurative language is used in the first sentence of paragraph 9?
   a. No figurative language is used in the first sentence of paragraph 9
   b. Simile
   c. Metaphor
   d. Hyperbole

41. From what point of view is this article written?
   a. First person
   b. Second person
   c. Third person
   d. All of the above

42. Which of the following best describes the theme of this article?
   a. Hang gliding has a rich history that began in the 1890s with two inventors
   b. Modern hang gliding has come far and is a safe, fun way to soar through the sky
   c. Hang gliders are 13 to 28 feet wide and have a sturdy frame and harness or seat
   d. The modern hang glider premiered at a meet in California in 1971

43. What material is used to make modern hang glider frames?
   a. Aluminum
   b. Steel
   c. Wood
   d. PVC

44. Who invented the first hang glider in 1891?
   a. Percy Picher
   b. The Wright brothers
   c. Donald Regalo
   d. Otto Lilienthal

45. Which of the following is a main idea in this article?
   a. Modern glider sails are 13 to 28 feet wide
   b. Glider pilots must know the rules of the sky
   c. All glider pilots should wear helmets for safety
   d. Modern glider design premiered in 1971

46. How did World War II positively impact the sport of hang gliding?
   a. It did not positively impact the sport of hang gliding
   b. Gliders were used in World War II in Europe and Asia
   c. Returning military pilots wanted to fly but couldn't afford planes
   d. Flight had become much safer due to World War II technology

47. What is the minimum sustained wind speed for a hang glider pilot to take off without running?
   a. 12 mph
   b. 21 mph
   c. 33 mph
   d. 47 mph

48. How far away from airports should hang glider pilots stay while flying?
   a. 100 feet
   b. 500 feet
   c. 1 mile
   d. 5 miles

Answers and Explanations

1. B: is the best choice because it offers the best definition of test anxiety according to the article. A, C, and D are not the best choices because they do not give accurate definitions of test anxiety according to the article.

2. A: is the best choice because it is the best explanation of a mnemonic device. B, C, and D are not the best choices because they are not clear and appropriate explanations of mnemonic devices.

3. D: is the best choice because the main purpose of this article is to identify potential solutions for test anxiety. A, B, and C are not the best choices because they do not identify the main purpose of the article.

4. C: is the best choice because the general tone of this article is informative. A, B, and D are not the best choices because the tone of the article is not entertaining, persuasive, or fictional.

5. A: is the best choice because it offers the clearest summary of the article. B, C, and D are not the best choices because they do not offer clear and complete summaries of the article.

6. C: is the best choice because according to paragraph 3, last-minute studying should be avoided. A, B, and D are not the best choices because they are not mentioned in paragraph 3 as study habits that should be avoided.

7. A: is the best choice because the first step to reducing test anxiety is better study habits. B, C, and D are not the best choices because they do not identify the first step to reducing test anxiety.

8. B: is the best choice because the third step to reducing test anxiety is positive self-talk. A, C, and D are not the best choices because they do not represent the third step to reducing test anxiety.

9. D: is the best choice because it is the only answer choice that is a supporting detail. A, B, and C are not the best choices because they are all main ideas in the article, not supporting details.

10. C: is the best choice because this article is organized in a problem-and-solution format. A, B, and D are not the best choices because this article is not organized in an inverted pyramid, proposition-and-support, or simple exposition format.

11. D: is the best choice because the two specific relaxation techniques mentioned in the article are visualization and deep breathing. A, B, and C are not the best choices because they do not reflect the two specific relaxation techniques discussed in this article.

12. B: is the best choice because paragraph 8 discusses the "final key" to overcoming test anxiety. A, C, and D are not the best choices because paragraphs 6, 7, and 9 do not discuss the "final key" to overcoming test anxiety.

13. C: is the best choice because "sneaky" is the best synonym for "stealthy." A, B, and D are not the best choices because "evil," "careful," and "thick" are not good synonyms for "stealthy" as it is used in this poem.

14. A: is the best choice because line 5 uses personification, suggesting that the fog has an "eerie whisper." B, C, and D are not the best choices because metaphor, simile, and hyperbole are not used in line 5.

15. B: is the best choice because it most accurately describes what the poet accomplishes through the use of figurative language. A, C, and D are not the best choices because they do not clearly describe what the poet accomplishes in this poem through the use of figurative language.

16. D: is the best choice because in line 2, the fog is compared to a "dense, gray blanket." A, B, and C are not the best choices because in line 2, the fog is not compared to a whisper, the sea, or a shadow.

17. D: is the best choice because the rhyming pattern of this poem is AABB CCDD EEFF GG. A, B, and C are not the best choices because they do not accurately represent the rhyming pattern of this poem.

18. B: is the best choice because the metaphor in lines 3 and 4 clearly refers to grasses waving in the wind. A, C, and D are not the best choices because they do not reflect the correct subject of the metaphor in lines 3 and 4.

19. A: is the best choice because lines 13 and 14 contain a simile comparing the dragonflies to "scattered thoughts and fleeting dreams." B, C, and D are not the best choices because lines 13 and 14 do not contain a metaphor, hyperbole, or personification.

20. C: is the best choice because in line 17, "tacit" means silent. A, B, and D are not the best choices because in line 17, "tacit" does not mean beautiful, lazy, or bored.

21. B: is the best choice because the mood of this poem is quiet and peaceful. A, C, and D are not the best choices because they do not accurately represent the mood of this poem.

22. C: is the best choice because this poem contains 3 stanzas. A, B, and D are not the best choices because the poem does not have 1, 8, or 24 stanzas.

23. A: is the best choice because the general theme of both poems is nature. B, C, and D are not the best choices because the general theme of these two poems is not water, emotions, or time.

24. D: is the best choice because the most important difference between the styles of these two poems is that one is rhymed and the other is free verse. A, B, and C are not the best choices because they do not represent the most important difference between these two poems.

25. B: is the best choice because "scattered across" is the best definition of "littered" as it is used in paragraph 4. A, C, and D are not the best choices because they are not clear and accurate definitions of "littered" as it is used in paragraph 4.

26. A: is the best choice because the main setting for this story is Grandma Ruth's attic. B, C, and D are not the best choices because the main setting of this story is not the Goodwill store, Kevin's house, or Grandma Ruth's dining room.

27. C: is the best choice because "fewer and smaller" is a good definition for "sparser" as it is used in paragraph 15. A, B, and D are not the best choices because they are not clear and accurate definitions of "sparser" as it is used in paragraph 15.

28. C: is the best choice because this story is written in third-person point of view. A and B are not the best choices because the story is not written in first-person or second-person point of view. D is not the best choice because the story is written in third-person point of view.

29. D: is the best choice because in paragraph 15 the piles are compared to mole hills using "like," making the comparison a simile. A, B, and C are not the best choices because paragraph 15 does not use a metaphor, personification, or hyperbole.

30. C: is the best choice because the general theme of this story is "do the right thing." A, B, and D are not the best choices because they do not accurately represent the general theme of this story.

31. D: is the best choice because paragraph 25 contains the climax of the story, when Kevin must decide whether he will use his money for the quilt or save it for his bike. A, B, and C are not the best choices because the climax of the story is not found in paragraphs 12, 16, or 24.

32. A: is the best choice because it best represents why the quilt was so valuable to Grandma Ruth. B, C, and D are not the best choices because they do not accurately reflect why the quilt was valuable to Grandma Ruth.

33. B: is the best choice because it is the only option that is a supporting detail. A, C, and D are not the best choices because they are all main ideas instead of supporting details.

34. B: is the best choice because it is the most clear and accurate summary of the story. A, C, and D are not the best choices because they are not clear and accurate summaries of the story.

35. A: is the best choice because it is the only option that was not a part of Grandma Ruth's memory quilt. B, C, and D are not the best choices because they are all elements that were part of Grandma Ruth's memory quilt.

36. D: is the best choice because hyperbole is used at the end of paragraph 18. A, B, and C are not the best choices because paragraph 18 does not contain simile, metaphor, or personification.

37. B: is the best choice because in paragraph 3, "advent" means beginning. A, C, and D are not the best choices because in paragraph 3, "advent" does not mean end, expansion, or popularity.

38. D: is the best choice because in this article, "thermals" are warm air currents that lift gliders. A, B, and C are not the best choices because they do not offer correct definitions of "thermals" as it is used in this article.

39. A: is the best choice because the author's main purpose in writing this article is to inform. B, C, and D are not the best choices because the author's main purpose is not to entertain, analyze, or persuade.

40. C: is the best choice because the first sentence of paragraph 9 uses a metaphor to compare the sky to a canvas. A is not the best choice because figurative language is used in the first sentence of paragraph 9. B and D are not the best choices because the first sentence of paragraph 9 does not include a simile or hyperbole.

41. C: is the best choice because this article is written in third-person point of view. A and B are not the best choices because this article is not written in first-person or second-person point of view. D is not the best choice because this article is only written from one point of view: third person.

42. B: is the best choice because it offers the most accurate description of the theme of the article. A, C, and D are not the best choices because they do not accurately and completely describe the theme of the article.

43. A: is the best choice because modern hang glider frames are made from aluminum. B, C, and D are not the best choices because modern hang glider frames are not made from steel, wood, or PVC.

44. D: is the best choice because Otto Lilienthal invented the first hang glider in 1891. A, B, and C are not the best choices because the first hang glider was not invented by Percy Picher, the Wright brothers, or Donald Regalo.

45. B: is the best choice because it is the only option that represents a main idea of the article. A, C, and D are not the best choices because they are all supporting details, not main ideas of the article.

46. C: is the best choice because it correctly explains how World War II positively impacted the sport of hang gliding. A is not the best choice because World War II did positively impact the sport of hang gliding. B and D are not the best choices because they do not correctly explain World War II's positive impact on hang gliding.

47. A: is the best choice because the minimum sustained wind speed for a glider pilot to take off without running is 12 mph. B, C, and D are not the best choices because the minimum sustained wind speed for a glider pilot to take off without running is not 21 mph, 33 mph, or 47 mph.

48. D: is the best choice because hang glider pilots should stay five miles away from airports while flying. A, B, and C are not the best choices because they do not accurately represent how far glider pilots should stay away from airports while flying.

Secret Key #1 - Time is Your Greatest Enemy

Pace Yourself

Wear a watch. At the beginning of the test, check the time (or start a chronometer on your watch to count the minutes), and check the time after every few questions to make sure you are "on schedule."

If you are forced to speed up, do it efficiently. Usually one or more answer choices can be eliminated without too much difficulty. Above all, don't panic. Don't speed up and just begin guessing at random choices. By pacing yourself, and continually monitoring your progress against your watch, you will always know exactly how far ahead or behind you are with your available time. If you find that you are one minute behind on the test, don't skip one question without spending any time on it, just to catch back up. Take 15 fewer seconds on the next four questions, and after four questions you'll have caught back up. Once you catch back up, you can continue working each problem at your normal pace.

Furthermore, don't dwell on the problems that you were rushed on. If a problem was taking up too much time and you made a hurried guess, it must be difficult. The difficult questions are the ones you are most likely to miss anyway, so it isn't a big loss. It is better to end with more time than you need than to run out of time.

Lastly, sometimes it is beneficial to slow down if you are constantly getting ahead of time. You are always more likely to catch a careless mistake by working more slowly than quickly, and among very high-scoring test takers (those who are likely to have lots of time left over), careless errors affect the score more than mastery of material.

Secret Key #2 - Guessing is not Guesswork

You probably know that guessing is a good idea - unlike other standardized tests, there is no penalty for getting a wrong answer. Even if you have no idea about a question, you still have a 20-25% chance of getting it right.

Most test takers do not understand the impact that proper guessing can have on their score. Unless you score extremely high, guessing will significantly contribute to your final score.

Monkeys Take the Test

What most test takers don't realize is that to insure that 20-25% chance, you have to guess randomly. If you put 20 monkeys in a room to take this test, assuming they answered once per question and behaved themselves, on average they would get 20-25% of the questions correct. Put 20 test takers in the room, and the average will be much lower among guessed questions. Why?

1. The test writers intentionally write deceptive answer choices that "look" right. A test taker has no idea about a question, so picks the "best looking" answer, which is often

wrong. The monkey has no idea what looks good and what doesn't, so will consistently be lucky about 20-25% of the time.

2. Test takers will eliminate answer choices from the guessing pool based on a hunch or intuition. Simple but correct answers often get excluded, leaving a 0% chance of being correct. The monkey has no clue, and often gets lucky with the best choice.

This is why the process of elimination endorsed by most test courses is flawed and detrimental to your performance- test takers don't guess, they make an ignorant stab in the dark that is usually worse than random.

$5 Challenge

Let me introduce one of the most valuable ideas of this course- the $5 challenge:

You only mark your "best guess" if you are willing to bet $5 on it.
You only eliminate choices from guessing if you are willing to bet $5 on it.

Why $5? Five dollars is an amount of money that is small yet not insignificant, and can really add up fast (20 questions could cost you $100). Likewise, each answer choice on one question of the test will have a small impact on your overall score, but it can really add up to a lot of points in the end.

The process of elimination IS valuable. The following shows your chance of guessing it right:

If you eliminate wrong answer choices until only this many remain:	Chance of getting it correct:
1	100%
2	50%
3	33%

However, if you accidentally eliminate the right answer or go on a hunch for an incorrect answer, your chances drop dramatically: to 0%. By guessing among all the answer choices, you are GUARANTEED to have a shot at the right answer.

That's why the $5 test is so valuable- if you give up the advantage and safety of a pure guess, it had better be worth the risk.

What we still haven't covered is how to be sure that whatever guess you make is truly random. Here's the easiest way:

Always pick the first answer choice among those remaining.

Such a technique means that you have decided, **before you see a single test question**, exactly how you are going to guess- and since the order of choices tells you nothing about which one is correct, this guessing technique is perfectly random.

This section is not meant to scare you away from making educated guesses or eliminating choices- you just need to define when a choice is worth eliminating. The $5 test, along with a pre-defined random guessing strategy, is the best way to make sure you reap all of the benefits of guessing.

Secret Key #3 - Practice Smarter, Not Harder

Many test takers delay the test preparation process because they dread the awful amounts of practice time they think necessary to succeed on the test. We have refined an effective method that will take you only a fraction of the time.

There are a number of "obstacles" in your way to succeed. Among these are answering questions, finishing in time, and mastering test-taking strategies. All must be executed on the day of the test at peak performance, or your score will suffer. The test is a mental marathon that has a large impact on your future.

Just like a marathon runner, it is important to work your way up to the full challenge. So first you just worry about questions, and then time, and finally strategy:

Success Strategy

1. Find a good source for practice tests.
2. If you are willing to make a larger time investment, consider using more than one study guide- often the different approaches of multiple authors will help you "get" difficult concepts.
3. Take a practice test with no time constraints, with all study helps "open book." Take your time with questions and focus on applying strategies.
4. Take a practice test with time constraints, with all guides "open book."
5. Take a final practice test with no open material and time limits

If you have time to take more practice tests, just repeat step 5. By gradually exposing yourself to the full rigors of the test environment, you will condition your mind to the stress of test day and maximize your success.

Secret Key #4 - Prepare, Don't Procrastinate

Let me state an obvious fact: if you take the test three times, you will get three different scores. This is due to the way you feel on test day, the level of preparedness you have, and, despite the test writers' claims to the contrary, some tests WILL be easier for you than others.

Since your future depends so much on your score, you should maximize your chances of success. In order to maximize the likelihood of success, you've got to prepare in advance. This means taking practice tests and spending time learning the information and test taking strategies you will need to succeed.

Never take the test as a "practice" test, expecting that you can just take it again if you need to. Feel free to take sample tests on your own, but when you go to take the official test, be prepared, be focused, and do your best the first time!

Secret Key #5 - Test Yourself

Everyone knows that time is money. There is no need to spend too much of your time or too little of your time preparing for the test. You should only spend as much of your precious time preparing as is necessary for you to get the score you need.

Once you have taken a practice test under real conditions of time constraints, then you will know if you are ready for the test or not.

If you have scored extremely high the first time that you take the practice test, then there is not much point in spending countless hours studying. You are already there.

Benchmark your abilities by retaking practice tests and seeing how much you have improved. Once you score high enough to guarantee success, then you are ready.

If you have scored well below where you need, then knuckle down and begin studying in earnest. Check your improvement regularly through the use of practice tests under real conditions. Above all, don't worry, panic, or give up. The key is perseverance!

Then, when you go to take the test, remain confident and remember how well you did on the practice tests. If you can score high enough on a practice test, then you can do the same on the real thing.

General Strategies

The most important thing you can do is to ignore your fears and jump into the test immediately- do not be overwhelmed by any strange-sounding terms. You have to jump into the test like jumping into a pool- all at once is the easiest way.

Make Predictions

As you read and understand the question, try to guess what the answer will be. Remember that several of the answer choices are wrong, and once you begin reading them, your mind will immediately become cluttered with answer choices designed to throw you off. Your mind is typically the most focused immediately after you have read the question and digested its contents. If you can, try to predict what the correct answer will be. You may be surprised at what you can predict.

Quickly scan the choices and see if your prediction is in the listed answer choices. If it is, then you can be quite confident that you have the right answer. It still won't hurt to check the other answer choices, but most of the time, you've got it!

Answer the Question

It may seem obvious to only pick answer choices that answer the question, but the test writers can create some excellent answer choices that are wrong. Don't pick an answer just because it sounds right, or you believe it to be true. It MUST answer the question. Once you've made your selection, always go back and check it against the question and make sure that you didn't misread the question, and the answer choice does answer the question posed.

Benchmark

After you read the first answer choice, decide if you think it sounds correct or not. If it doesn't, move on to the next answer choice. If it does, mentally mark that answer choice. This doesn't mean that you've definitely selected it as your answer choice, it just means that it's the best you've seen thus far. Go ahead and read the next choice. If the next choice is worse than the one you've already selected, keep going to the next answer choice. If the next choice is better than the choice you've already selected, mentally mark the new answer choice as your best guess.

The first answer choice that you select becomes your standard. Every other answer choice must be benchmarked against that standard. That choice is correct until proven otherwise by another answer choice beating it out. Once you've decided that no other answer choice seems as good, do one final check to ensure that your answer choice answers the question posed.

Valid Information

Don't discount any of the information provided in the question. Every piece of information may be necessary to determine the correct answer. None of the information in the question is there to throw you off (while the answer choices will certainly have information to throw you off). If two seemingly unrelated topics are discussed, don't ignore either. You can be confident there is a relationship, or it wouldn't be included in the question, and you are probably going to have to determine what is that relationship to find the answer.

Avoid "Fact Traps"

Don't get distracted by a choice that is factually true. Your search is for the answer that answers the question. Stay focused and don't fall for an answer that is true but incorrect. Always go back to the question and make sure you're choosing an answer that actually answers the question and is not just a true statement. An answer can be factually correct, but it MUST answer the question asked. Additionally, two answers can both be seemingly correct, so be sure to read all of the answer choices, and make sure that you get the one that BEST answers the question.

Milk the Question

Some of the questions may throw you completely off. They might deal with a subject you have not been exposed to, or one that you haven't reviewed in years. While your lack of knowledge about the subject will be a hindrance, the question itself can give you many clues that will help you find the correct answer. Read the question carefully and look for clues. Watch particularly for adjectives and nouns describing difficult terms or words that you don't recognize. Regardless of if you completely understand a word or not, replacing it with a synonym either provided or one you more familiar with may help you to understand what the questions are asking. Rather than wracking your mind about specific detailed information concerning a difficult term or word, try to use mental substitutes that are easier to understand.

The Trap of Familiarity

Don't just choose a word because you recognize it. On difficult questions, you may not recognize a number of words in the answer choices. The test writers don't put "make-believe" words on the test; so don't think that just because you only recognize all the words in one answer choice means that answer choice must be correct. If you only recognize words in one answer choice, then focus on that one. Is it correct? Try your best to determine if it is correct. If it is, that is great, but if it doesn't, eliminate it. Each word and answer choice you eliminate increases your chances of getting the question correct, even if you then have to guess among the unfamiliar choices.

Eliminate Answers

Eliminate choices as soon as you realize they are wrong. But be careful! Make sure you consider all of the possible answer choices. Just because one appears right, doesn't mean that the next one won't be even better! The test writers will usually put more than one good answer choice for every question, so read all of them. Don't worry if you are stuck between two that seem right. By getting down to just two remaining possible choices, your odds are now 50/50. Rather than wasting too much time, play the odds. You are guessing, but guessing wisely, because you've been able to knock out some of the answer choices that you know are wrong. If you are eliminating choices and realize that the last answer choice you are left with is also obviously wrong, don't panic. Start over and consider each choice again. There may easily be something that you missed the first time and will realize on the second pass.

Tough Questions

If you are stumped on a problem or it appears too hard or too difficult, don't waste time. Move on! Remember though, if you can quickly check for obviously incorrect answer choices, your chances of guessing correctly are greatly improved. Before you completely give up, at least try to knock out a couple of possible answers. Eliminate what you can and then guess at the remaining answer choices before moving on.

Brainstorm

If you get stuck on a difficult question, spend a few seconds quickly brainstorming. Run through the complete list of possible answer choices. Look at each choice and ask yourself, "Could this answer the question satisfactorily?" Go through each answer choice and consider it independently of the other. By systematically going through all possibilities, you may find something that you would otherwise overlook. Remember that when you get stuck, it's important to try to keep moving.

Read Carefully

Understand the problem. Read the question and answer choices carefully. Don't miss the question because you misread the terms. You have plenty of time to read each question thoroughly and make sure you understand what is being asked. Yet a happy medium must be attained, so don't waste too much time. You must read carefully, but efficiently.

Face Value

When in doubt, use common sense. Always accept the situation in the problem at face value. Don't read too much into it. These problems will not require you to make huge leaps of logic. The test writers aren't trying to throw you off with a cheap trick. If you have to go beyond creativity and make a leap of logic in order to have an answer choice answer the question, then you should look at the other answer choices. Don't overcomplicate the problem by creating theoretical relationships or explanations that will warp time or space. These are normal problems rooted in reality. It's just that the applicable relationship or explanation may not be readily apparent and you have to figure things out. Use your common sense to interpret anything that isn't clear.

Prefixes

If you're having trouble with a word in the question or answer choices, try dissecting it. Take advantage of every clue that the word might include. Prefixes and suffixes can be a huge help. Usually they allow you to determine a basic meaning. Pre- means before, post-means after, pro - is positive, de- is negative. From these prefixes and suffixes, you can get an idea of the general meaning of the word and try to put it into context. Beware though of any traps. Just because con is the opposite of pro, doesn't necessarily mean congress is the opposite of progress!

Hedge Phrases

Watch out for critical "hedge" phrases, such as likely, may, can, will often, sometimes, often, almost, mostly, usually, generally, rarely, sometimes. Question writers insert these hedge phrases to cover every possibility. Often an answer choice will be wrong simply because it leaves no room for exception. Avoid answer choices that have definitive words like "exactly," and "always".

Switchback Words

Stay alert for "switchbacks". These are the words and phrases frequently used to alert you to shifts in thought. The most common switchback word is "but". Others include although, however, nevertheless, on the other hand, even though, while, in spite of, despite, regardless of.

New Information

Correct answer choices will rarely have completely new information included. Answer choices typically are straightforward reflections of the material asked about and will directly relate to the question. If a new piece of information is included in an answer choice that doesn't even seem to relate to the topic being asked about, then that answer choice is likely incorrect. All of the information needed to answer the question is usually provided for you, and so you should not have to make guesses that are unsupported or choose answer choices that require unknown information that cannot be reasoned on its own.

Time Management

On technical questions, don't get lost on the technical terms. Don't spend too much time on any one question. If you don't know what a term means, then since you don't have a dictionary, odds are you aren't going to get much further. You should immediately recognize terms as whether or not you know them. If you don't, work with the other clues that you have, the other answer choices and terms provided, but don't waste too much time trying to figure out a difficult term.

Contextual Clues

Look for contextual clues. An answer can be right but not correct. The contextual clues will help you find the answer that is most right and is correct. Understand the context in which a phrase or statement is made. This will help you make important distinctions.

Don't Panic

Panicking will not answer any questions for you. Therefore, it isn't helpful. When you first see the question, if your mind goes blank, take a deep breath. Force yourself to mechanically go through the steps of solving the problem and using the strategies you've learned.

Pace Yourself

Don't get clock fever. It's easy to be overwhelmed when you're looking at a page full of questions, your mind is full of random thoughts and feeling confused, and the clock is ticking down faster than you would like. Calm down and maintain the pace that you have set for yourself. As long as you are on track by monitoring your pace, you are guaranteed to have enough time for yourself. When you get to the last few minutes of the test, it may seem like you won't have enough time left, but if you only have as many questions as you should have left at that point, then you're right on track!

Answer Selection

The best way to pick an answer choice is to eliminate all of those that are wrong, until only one is left and confirm that is the correct answer. Sometimes though, an answer choice may immediately look right. Be careful! Take a second to make sure that the other choices are not equally obvious. Don't make a hasty mistake. There are only two times that you should stop before checking other answers. First is when you are positive that the answer choice you have selected is correct. Second is when time is almost out and you have to make a quick guess!

Check Your Work

Since you will probably not know every term listed and the answer to every question, it is important that you get credit for the ones that you do know. Don't miss any questions through careless mistakes. If at all possible, try to take a second to look back over your answer selection and make sure you've selected the correct answer choice and haven't made a costly careless mistake (such as marking an answer choice that you didn't mean to mark). This quick double check should more than pay for itself in caught mistakes for the time it costs.

Beware of Directly Quoted Answers

Sometimes an answer choice will repeat word for word a portion of the question or reference section. However, beware of such exact duplication – it may be a trap! More than likely, the correct choice will paraphrase or summarize a point, rather than being exactly the same wording.

Slang

Scientific sounding answers are better than slang ones. An answer choice that begins "To compare the outcomes..." is much more likely to be correct than one that begins "Because some people insisted..."

Extreme Statements

Avoid wild answers that throw out highly controversial ideas that are proclaimed as established fact. An answer choice that states the "process should be used in certain situations, if..." is much more likely to be correct than one that states the "process should be discontinued completely." The first is a calm rational statement and doesn't even make a definitive, uncompromising stance, using a hedge word "if" to provide wiggle room, whereas the second choice is a radical idea and far more extreme.

Answer Choice Families

When you have two or more answer choices that are direct opposites or parallels, one of them is usually the correct answer. For instance, if one answer choice states "x increases" and another answer choice states "x decreases" or "y increases," then those two or three answer choices are very similar in construction and fall into the same family of answer choices. A family of answer choices is when two or three answer choices are very similar in construction, and yet often have a directly opposite meaning. Usually the correct answer choice will be in that family of answer choices. The "odd man out" or answer choice that doesn't seem to fit the parallel construction of the other answer choices is more likely to be incorrect.

Top 20 Test Taking Tips

1. Carefully follow all the test registration procedures
2. Know the test directions, duration, topics, question types, how many questions
3. Setup a flexible study schedule at least 3-4 weeks before test day
4. Study during the time of day you are most alert, relaxed, and stress free
5. Maximize your learning style; visual learner use visual study aids, auditory learner use auditory study aids
6. Focus on your weakest knowledge base
7. Find a study partner to review with and help clarify questions
8. Practice, practice, practice
9. Get a good night's sleep; don't try to cram the night before the test
10. Eat a well balanced meal
11. Know the exact physical location of the testing site; drive the route to the site prior to test day
12. Bring a set of ear plugs; the testing center could be noisy
13. Wear comfortable, loose fitting, layered clothing to the testing center; prepare for it to be either cold or hot during the test
14. Bring at least 2 current forms of ID to the testing center
15. Arrive to the test early; be prepared to wait and be patient
16. Eliminate the obviously wrong answer choices, then guess the first remaining choice
17. Pace yourself; don't rush, but keep working and move on if you get stuck
18. Maintain a positive attitude even if the test is going poorly
19. Keep your first answer unless you are positive it is wrong
20. Check your work, don't make a careless mistake

Special Report: What Your Test Score Will Tell You About Your IQ

Did you know that most standardized tests correlate very strongly with IQ? In fact, your general intelligence is a better predictor of your success than any other factor, and most tests intentionally measure this trait to some degree to ensure that those selected by the test are truly qualified for the test's purposes.

Before we can delve into the relation between your test score and IQ, I will first have to explain what exactly is IQ. Here's the formula:

Your IQ = 100 + (Number of standard deviations below or above the average)*15

Now, let's define standard deviations by using an example. If we have 5 people with 5 different heights, then first we calculate the average. Let's say the average was 65 inches. The standard deviation is the "average distance" away from the average of each of the members. It is a direct measure of variability - if the 5 people included Jackie Chan and Shaquille O'Neal, obviously there's a lot more variability in that group than a group of 5 sisters who are all within 6 inches in height of each other. The standard deviation uses a number to characterize the average range of difference within a group.

A convenient feature of most groups is that they have a "normal" distribution- makes sense that most things would be normal, right? Without getting into a bunch of statistical mumbo-jumbo, you just need to know that if you know the average of the group and the standard deviation, you can successfully predict someone's percentile rank in the group.

Confused? Let me give you an example. If instead of 5 people's heights, we had 100 people, we could figure out their rank in height JUST by knowing the average, standard deviation, and their height. We wouldn't need to know each person's height and manually rank them, we could just predict their rank based on three numbers.

What this means is that you can take your PERCENTILE rank that is often given with your test and relate this to your RELATIVE IQ of people taking the test - that is, your IQ relative to the people taking the test. Obviously, there's no way to know your actual IQ because the people taking a standardized test are usually not very good samples of the general population- many of those with extremely low IQ's never achieve a level of success or competency necessary to complete a typical standardized test. In fact, professional psychologists who measure IQ actually have to use non-written tests that can fairly measure the IQ of those not able to complete a traditional test.

The bottom line is to not take your test score too seriously, but it is fun to compute your "relative IQ" among the people who took the test with you. I've done the calculations below. Just look up your percentile rank in the left and then you'll see your "relative IQ" for your test in the right hand column-

Percentile Rank	Your Relative IQ		Percentile Rank	Your Relative IQ
99	135		59	103
98	131		58	103
97	128		57	103
96	126		56	102
95	125		55	102
94	123		54	102
93	122		53	101
92	121		52	101
91	120		51	100
90	119		50	100
89	118		49	100
88	118		48	99
87	117		47	99
86	116		46	98
85	116		45	98
84	115		44	98
83	114		43	97
82	114		42	97
81	113		41	97
80	113		40	96
79	112		39	96
78	112		38	95
77	111		37	95
76	111		36	95
75	110		35	94
74	110		34	94
73	109		33	93
72	109		32	93
71	108		31	93
70	108		30	92
69	107		29	92
68	107		28	91
67	107		27	91
66	106		26	90
65	106		25	90
64	105		24	89
63	105		23	89
62	105		22	88
61	104		21	88
60	104		20	87

Special Report: What is Test Anxiety and How to Overcome It?

The very nature of tests caters to some level of anxiety, nervousness or tension, just as we feel for any important event that occurs in our lives. A little bit of anxiety or nervousness can be a good thing. It helps us with motivation, and makes achievement just that much sweeter. However, too much anxiety can be a problem; especially if it hinders our ability to function and perform.

"Test anxiety," is the term that refers to the emotional reactions that some test-takers experience when faced with a test or exam. Having a fear of testing and exams is based upon a rational fear, since the test-taker's performance can shape the course of an academic career. Nevertheless, experiencing excessive fear of examinations will only interfere with the test-takers ability to perform, and his/her chances to be successful.

There are a large variety of causes that can contribute to the development and sensation of test anxiety. These include, but are not limited to lack of performance and worrying about issues surrounding the test.

Lack of Preparation

Lack of preparation can be identified by the following behaviors or situations:

Not scheduling enough time to study, and therefore cramming the night before the test or exam
Managing time poorly, to create the sensation that there is not enough time to do everything
Failing to organize the text information in advance, so that the study material consists of the entire text and not simply the pertinent information
Poor overall studying habits

Worrying, on the other hand, can be related to both the test taker, or many other factors around him/her that will be affected by the results of the test. These include worrying about:

Previous performances on similar exams, or exams in general
How friends and other students are achieving
The negative consequences that will result from a poor grade or failure

There are three primary elements to test anxiety. Physical components, which involve the same typical bodily reactions as those to acute anxiety (to be discussed below). Emotional factors have to do with fear or panic. Mental or cognitive issues concerning attention spans and memory abilities.

Physical Signals

There are many different symptoms of test anxiety, and these are not limited to mental and emotional strain. Frequently there are a range of physical signals that will let a test taker know that he/she is suffering from test anxiety. These bodily changes can include the following:

Perspiring
Sweaty palms
Wet, trembling hands
Nausea
Dry mouth
A knot in the stomach
Headache
Faintness
Muscle tension
Aching shoulders, back and neck
Rapid heart beat
Feeling too hot/cold

To recognize the sensation of test anxiety, a test-taker should monitor him/herself for the following sensations:

The physical distress symptoms as listed above
Emotional sensitivity, expressing emotional feelings such as the need to cry or laugh too much, or a sensation of anger or helplessness
A decreased ability to think, causing the test-taker to blank out or have racing thoughts that are hard to organize or control.

Though most students will feel some level of anxiety when faced with a test or exam, the majority can cope with that anxiety and maintain it at a manageable level. However, those who cannot are faced with a very real and very serious condition, which can and should be controlled for the immeasurable benefit of this sufferer.

Naturally, these sensations lead to negative results for the testing experience. The most common effects of test anxiety have to do with nervousness and mental blocking.

Nervousness

Nervousness can appear in several different levels:

The test-taker's difficulty, or even inability to read and understand the questions on the test
The difficulty or inability to organize thoughts to a coherent form
The difficulty or inability to recall key words and concepts relating to the testing questions (especially essays)
The receipt of poor grades on a test, though the test material was well known by the test taker

Conversely, a person may also experience mental blocking, which involves:

Blanking out on test questions
Only remembering the correct answers to the questions when the test has already finished.

Fortunately for test anxiety sufferers, beating these feelings, to a large degree, has to do with proper preparation. When a test taker has a feeling of preparedness, then anxiety will be dramatically lessened.

The first step to resolving anxiety issues is to distinguish which of the two types of anxiety are being suffered. If the anxiety is a direct result of a lack of preparation, this should be considered a normal reaction, and the anxiety level (as opposed to the test results) shouldn't be anything to worry about. However, if, when adequately prepared, the test-taker still panics, blanks out, or seems to overreact, this is not a fully rational reaction. While this can be considered normal too, there are many ways to combat and overcome these effects.

Remember that anxiety cannot be entirely eliminated, however, there are ways to minimize it, to make the anxiety easier to manage. Preparation is one of the best ways to minimize test anxiety. Therefore the following techniques are wise in order to best fight off any anxiety that may want to build.

To begin with, try to avoid cramming before a test, whenever it is possible. By trying to memorize an entire term's worth of information in one day, you'll be shocking your system, and not giving yourself a very good chance to absorb the information. This is an easy path to anxiety, so for those who suffer from test anxiety, cramming should not even be considered an option.

Instead of cramming, work throughout the semester to combine all of the material which is presented throughout the semester, and work on it gradually as the course goes by, making sure to master the main concepts first, leaving minor details for a week or so before the test.

To study for the upcoming exam, be sure to pose questions that may be on the examination, to gauge the ability to answer them by integrating the ideas from your texts, notes and lectures, as well as any supplementary readings.

If it is truly impossible to cover all of the information that was covered in that particular term, concentrate on the most important portions, that can be covered very well. Learn these concepts as best as possible, so that when the test comes, a goal can be made to use these concepts as presentations of your knowledge.

In addition to study habits, changes in attitude are critical to beating a struggle with test anxiety. In fact, an improvement of the perspective over the entire test-taking experience can actually help a test taker to enjoy studying and therefore improve the overall experience. Be certain not to overemphasize the significance of the grade - know that the result of the test is neither a reflection of self worth, nor is it a measure of intelligence; one grade will not predict a person's future success.

To improve an overall testing outlook, the following steps should be tried:

Keeping in mind that the most reasonable expectation for taking a test is to expect to try to demonstrate as much of what you know as you possibly can.
Reminding ourselves that a test is only one test; this is not the only one, and there will be others.
The thought of thinking of oneself in an irrational, all-or-nothing term should be avoided at all costs.
A reward should be designated for after the test, so there's something to look forward to. Whether it be going to a movie, going out to eat, or simply visiting friends, schedule it in advance, and do it no matter what result is expected on the exam.

Test-takers should also keep in mind that the basics are some of the most important things, even beyond anti-anxiety techniques and studying. Never neglect the basic social, emotional and biological needs, in order to try to absorb information. In order to best achieve, these three factors must be held as just as important as the studying itself.

Study Steps

Remember the following important steps for studying:

Maintain healthy nutrition and exercise habits. Continue both your recreational activities and social pass times. These both contribute to your physical and emotional well being.
Be certain to get a good amount of sleep, especially the night before the test, because when you're overtired you are not able to perform to the best of your best ability.
Keep the studying pace to a moderate level by taking breaks when they are needed, and varying the work whenever possible, to keep the mind fresh instead of getting bored. When enough studying has been done that all the material that can be learned has been learned, and the test taker is prepared for the test, stop studying and do something relaxing such as listening to music, watching a movie, or taking a warm bubble bath.

There are also many other techniques to minimize the uneasiness or apprehension that is experienced along with test anxiety before, during, or even after the examination. In fact, there are a great deal of things that can be done to stop anxiety from interfering with lifestyle and performance. Again, remember that anxiety will not be eliminated entirely, and it shouldn't be. Otherwise that "up" feeling for exams would not exist, and most of us depend on that sensation to perform better than usual. However, this anxiety has to be at a level that is manageable.

Of course, as we have just discussed, being prepared for the exam is half the battle right away. Attending all classes, finding out what knowledge will be expected on the exam, and knowing the exam schedules are easy steps to lowering anxiety. Keeping up with work will remove the need to cram, and efficient study habits will eliminate wasted time. Studying should be done in an ideal location for concentration, so that it is simple to become interested in the material and give it complete attention. A method such as SQ3R (Survey, Question, Read, Recite, Review) is a wonderful key to follow to make sure that the study habits are as effective as possible, especially in the case of learning from a textbook. Flashcards are great techniques for memorization. Learning to take good notes will mean that notes will be full of useful information, so that less sifting will need to be done to seek out what is pertinent for studying. Reviewing notes after class and then again on occasion will keep the information fresh in the mind. From notes that have been taken summary sheets and outlines can be made for simpler reviewing.

A study group can also be a very motivational and helpful place to study, as there will be a sharing of ideas, all of the minds can work together, to make sure that everyone understands, and the studying will be made more interesting because it will be a social occasion.

Basically, though, as long as the test-taker remains organized and self confident, with efficient study habits, less time will need to be spent studying, and higher grades will be achieved.

To become self confident, there are many useful steps. The first of these is "self talk." It has been shown through extensive research, that self-talk for students who suffer from test anxiety, should be well monitored, in order to make sure that it contributes to self confidence as opposed to sinking the student. Frequently the self talk of test-anxious students is negative or self-defeating, thinking that everyone else is smarter and faster, that they always mess up, and that if they don't do well, they'll fail the entire course. It is important to decreasing anxiety that awareness is made of self talk. Try writing any negative self thoughts and then disputing them with a positive statement instead. Begin self-encouragement as though it was a friend speaking. Repeat positive statements to help reprogram the mind to believing in successes instead of failures.

Helpful Techniques

Other extremely helpful techniques include:

Self-visualization of doing well and reaching goals
While aiming for an "A" level of understanding, don't try to "overprotect" by setting your expectations lower. This will only convince the mind to stop studying in order to meet the lower expectations.
Don't make comparisons with the results or habits of other students. These are individual factors, and different things work for different people, causing different results.
Strive to become an expert in learning what works well, and what can be done in order to improve. Consider collecting this data in a journal.
Create rewards for after studying instead of doing things before studying that will only turn into avoidance behaviors.
Make a practice of relaxing - by using methods such as progressive relaxation, self-hypnosis, guided imagery, etc - in order to make relaxation an automatic sensation.
Work on creating a state of relaxed concentration so that concentrating will take on the focus of the mind, so that none will be wasted on worrying.
Take good care of the physical self by eating well and getting enough sleep.
Plan in time for exercise and stick to this plan.

Beyond these techniques, there are other methods to be used before, during and after the test that will help the test-taker perform well in addition to overcoming anxiety.

Before the exam comes the academic preparation. This involves establishing a study schedule and beginning at least one week before the actual date of the test. By doing this, the anxiety of not having enough time to study for the test will be automatically eliminated. Moreover, this will make the studying a much more effective experience, ensuring that the learning will be an easier process. This relieves much undue pressure on the test-taker.

Summary sheets, note cards, and flash cards with the main concepts and examples of these main concepts should be prepared in advance of the actual studying time. A topic should never be eliminated from this process. By omitting a topic because it isn't expected to be on the test is only setting up the test-taker for anxiety should it actually appear on the exam. Utilize the course syllabus for laying out the topics that should be studied. Carefully go over the notes that were made in class, paying special attention to any of the issues that the professor took special care to emphasize while lecturing in class. In the textbooks, use the chapter review, or if possible, the chapter tests, to begin your review.

It may even be possible to ask the instructor what information will be covered on the exam, or what the format of the exam will be (for example, multiple choice, essay, free form, true-false). Additionally, see if it is possible to find out how many questions will be on the test. If a review sheet or sample test has been offered by the professor, make good use of it, above anything else, for the preparation for the test. Another great resource for getting to know the examination is reviewing tests from previous semesters. Use these tests to review, and aim to achieve a 100% score on each of the possible topics. With a few exceptions, the goal that you set for yourself is the highest one that you will reach.

Take all of the questions that were assigned as homework, and rework them to any other possible course material. The more problems reworked, the more skill and confidence will form as a result. When forming the solution to a problem, write out each of the steps. Don't simply do head work. By doing as many steps on paper as possible, much clarification and therefore confidence will be formed. Do this with as many homework problems as possible, before checking the answers. By checking the answer after each problem, a reinforcement will exist, that will not be on the exam. Study situations should be as exam-like as possible, to prime the test-taker's system for the experience. By waiting to check the answers at the end, a psychological advantage will be formed, to decrease the stress factor.

Another fantastic reason for not cramming is the avoidance of confusion in concepts, especially when it comes to mathematics. 8-10 hours of study will become one hundred percent more effective if it is spread out over a week or at least several days, instead of doing it all in one sitting. Recognize that the human brain requires time in order to assimilate new material, so frequent breaks and a span of study time over several days will be much more beneficial.

Additionally, don't study right up until the point of the exam. Studying should stop a minimum of one hour before the exam begins. This allows the brain to rest and put things in their proper order. This will also provide the time to become as relaxed as possible when going into the examination room. The test-taker will also have time to eat well and eat sensibly. Know that the brain needs food as much as the rest of the body. With enough food and enough sleep, as well as a relaxed attitude, the body and the mind are primed for success.

Avoid any anxious classmates who are talking about the exam. These students only spread anxiety, and are not worth sharing the anxious sentimentalities.

Before the test also involves creating a positive attitude, so mental preparation should also be a point of concentration. There are many keys to creating a positive attitude. Should fears become rushing in, make a visualization of taking the exam, doing well, and seeing an A written on the paper. Write out a list of affirmations that will bring a feeling of confidence, such as "I am doing well in my English class," "I studied well and know my material," "I enjoy this class." Even if the affirmations aren't believed at first, it sends a positive message to the subconscious which will result in an alteration of the overall belief system, which is the system that creates reality.

If a sensation of panic begins, work with the fear and imagine the very worst! Work through the entire scenario of not passing the test, failing the entire course, and dropping out of school, followed by not getting a job, and pushing a shopping cart through the dark alley where you'll live. This will place things into perspective! Then, practice deep breathing and create a visualization of the opposite situation - achieving an "A" on the exam, passing the entire course, receiving the degree at a graduation ceremony.

On the day of the test, there are many things to be done to ensure the best results, as well as the most calm outlook. The following stages are suggested in order to maximize test-taking potential:

Begin the examination day with a moderate breakfast, and avoid any coffee or beverages with caffeine if the test taker is prone to jitters. Even people who are used to managing caffeine can feel jittery or light-headed when it is taken on a test day.
Attempt to do something that is relaxing before the examination begins. As last minute cramming clouds the mastering of overall concepts, it is better to use this time to create a calming outlook.
Be certain to arrive at the test location well in advance, in order to provide time to select a location that is away from doors, windows and other distractions, as well as giving enough time to relax before the test begins.
Keep away from anxiety generating classmates who will upset the sensation of stability and relaxation that is being attempted before the exam.
Should the waiting period before the exam begins cause anxiety, create a self-distraction by reading a light magazine or something else that is relaxing and simple.

During the exam itself, read the entire exam from beginning to end, and find out how much time should be allotted to each individual problem. Once writing the exam, should more time be taken for a problem, it should be abandoned, in order to begin another problem. If there is time at the end, the unfinished problem can always be returned to and completed.

Read the instructions very carefully - twice - so that unpleasant surprises won't follow during or after the exam has ended.

When writing the exam, pretend that the situation is actually simply the completion of homework within a library, or at home. This will assist in forming a relaxed atmosphere, and will allow the brain extra focus for the complex thinking function.

Begin the exam with all of the questions with which the most confidence is felt. This will build the confidence level regarding the entire exam and will begin a quality momentum. This will also create encouragement for trying the problems where uncertainty resides.

Going with the "gut instinct" is always the way to go when solving a problem. Second guessing should be avoided at all costs. Have confidence in the ability to do well.

For essay questions, create an outline in advance that will keep the mind organized and make certain that all of the points are remembered. For multiple choice, read every answer, even if the correct one has been spotted - a better one may exist.

Continue at a pace that is reasonable and not rushed, in order to be able to work carefully. Provide enough time to go over the answers at the end, to check for small errors that can be corrected.

Should a feeling of panic begin, breathe deeply, and think of the feeling of the body releasing sand through its pores. Visualize a calm, peaceful place, and include all of the sights, sounds and sensations of this image. Continue the deep breathing, and take a few minutes to continue this with closed eyes. When all is well again, return to the test.

If a "blanking" occurs for a certain question, skip it and move on to the next question. There will be time to return to the other question later. Get everything done that can be done, first, to guarantee all the grades that can be compiled, and to build all of the confidence possible. Then return to the weaker questions to build the marks from there.

Remember, one's own reality can be created, so as long as the belief is there, success will follow. And remember: anxiety can happen later, right now, there's an exam to be written!

After the examination is complete, whether there is a feeling for a good grade or a bad grade, don't dwell on the exam, and be certain to follow through on the reward that was promised...and enjoy it! Don't dwell on any mistakes that have been made, as there is nothing that can be done at this point anyway.

Additionally, don't begin to study for the next test right away. Do something relaxing for a while, and let the mind relax and prepare itself to begin absorbing information again.

From the results of the exam - both the grade and the entire experience, be certain to learn from what has gone on. Perfect studying habits and work some more on confidence in order to make the next examination experience even better than the last one.

Learn to avoid places where openings occurred for laziness, procrastination and day dreaming.

Use the time between this exam and the next one to better learn to relax, even learning to relax on cue, so that any anxiety can be controlled during the next exam. Learn how to relax the body. Slouch in your chair if that helps. Tighten and then relax all of the different muscle groups, one group at a time, beginning with the feet and then working all the way up to the neck and face. This will ultimately relax the muscles more than they were to begin with. Learn how to breathe deeply and comfortably, and focus on this breathing going in and out as a relaxing thought. With every exhale, repeat the word "relax."

As common as test anxiety is, it is very possible to overcome it. Make yourself one of the test-takers who overcome this frustrating hindrance.

Special Report: Retaking the Test: What Are Your Chances at Improving Your Score?

After going through the experience of taking a major test, many test takers feel that once is enough. The test usually comes during a period of transition in the test taker's life, and taking the test is only one of a series of important events. With so many distractions and conflicting recommendations, it may be difficult for a test taker to rationally determine whether or not he should retake the test after viewing his scores.

The importance of the test usually only adds to the burden of the retake decision. However, don't be swayed by emotion. There a few simple questions that you can ask yourself to guide you as you try to determine whether a retake would improve your score:

1. What went wrong? Why wasn't your score what you expected?

Can you point to a single factor or problem that you feel caused the low score? Were you sick on test day? Was there an emotional upheaval in your life that caused a distraction? Were you late for the test or not able to use the full time allotment? If you can point to any of these specific, individual problems, then a retake should definitely be considered.

2. Is there enough time to improve?

Many problems that may show up in your score report may take a lot of time for improvement. A deficiency in a particular math skill may require weeks or months of tutoring and studying to improve. If you have enough time to improve an identified weakness, then a retake should definitely be considered.

3. How will additional scores be used? Will a score average, highest score, or most recent score be used?

Different test scores may be handled completely differently. If you've taken the test multiple times, sometimes your highest score is used, sometimes your average score is computed and used, and sometimes your most recent score is used. Make sure you understand what method will be used to evaluate your scores, and use that to help you determine whether a retake should be considered.

4. Are my practice test scores significantly higher than my actual test score?

If you have taken a lot of practice tests and are consistently scoring at a much higher level than your actual test score, then you should consider a retake. However, if you've taken five practice tests and only one of your scores was higher than your actual test score, or if your practice test scores were only slightly higher than your actual test score, then it is unlikely that you will significantly increase your score.

- 69 -

5. Do I need perfect scores or will I be able to live with this score? Will this score still allow me to follow my dreams?

What kind of score is acceptable to you? Is your current score "good enough?" Do you have to have a certain score in order to pursue the future of your dreams? If you won't be happy with your current score, and there's no way that you could live with it, then you should consider a retake. However, don't get your hopes up. If you are looking for significant improvement, that may or may not be possible. But if you won't be happy otherwise, it is at least worth the effort.

Remember that there are other considerations. To achieve your dream, it is likely that your grades may also be taken into account. A great test score is usually not the only thing necessary to succeed. Make sure that you aren't overemphasizing the importance of a high test score.

Furthermore, a retake does not always result in a higher score. Some test takers will score lower on a retake, rather than higher. One study shows that one-fourth of test takers will achieve a significant improvement in test score, while one-sixth of test takers will actually show a decrease. While this shows that most test takers will improve, the majority will only improve their scores a little and a retake may not be worth the test taker's effort.

Finally, if a test is taken only once and is considered in the added context of good grades on the part of a test taker, the person reviewing the grades and scores may be tempted to assume that the test taker just had a bad day while taking the test, and may discount the low test score in favor of the high grades. But if the test is retaken and the scores are approximately the same, then the validity of the low scores are only confirmed. Therefore, a retake could actually hurt a test taker by definitely bracketing a test taker's score ability to a limited range.

Special Report: Additional Bonus Material

Due to our efforts to try to keep this book to a manageable length, we've created a link that will give you access to all of your additional bonus material.

Please visit http://www.mometrix.com/bonus948/vsolg6read to access the information.